Ban the Book Report

Promoting Frequent and Enthusiastic Reading

Graham Foster

Pembroke Publishers Limited

© **2012 Pembroke Publishers**
538 Hood Road
Markham, Ontario, Canada L3R 3K9
www.pembrokepublishers.com

Distributed in the U.S. by Stenhouse Publishers
480 Congress Street
Portland, ME 04101
www.stenhouse.com

We acknowledge the financial support of the Government of Canada through the Book
Publishing Industry Development Program (BPIDP) for our publishing activities.

We acknowledge the assistance of the Government of Ontario through the Ontario
Media Development Corporation's Ontario Book Initiative.

Library and Archives Canada Cataloguing in Publication

Foster, Graham
    Ban the book report : promoting frequent and enthusiastic reading / Graham Foster.

Includes bibliographical references and index.
Issued also in electronic format.
ISBN 978-1-55138-264-7

    1. Reading. I. Title.

LB1050.F673 2012   418'.4071   C2012-903939-X

---

eBook format ISBN 978-1-55138-841-0

Editor: Kat Mototsune
Cover Design: John Zehethofer
Typesetting: Jay Tee Graphics Ltd.

Printed and bound in Canada
9 8 7 6 5 4 3 2 1

FSC
www.fsc.org
MIX
Paper from
responsible sources
FSC® C004071

Contents

Introduction

Powerful Alternatives to Book Reports

It's time to ban the book report! As we encourage students to read extensively, let's provide them with reading-response options that are more personally significant, more motivational, more varied, and more interesting than book reports.

Written book reports tend to be rigid and narrowly analytical, based on assigned topics, such as type of book, main character, summary, theme, and judgment of worth. Instead of requiring book reports about independent reading, wise teachers assign responses that more truly align with reasons that people spend quiet hours reading books: reading is a source of enjoyment and personal interest; it helps us sort out our beliefs and our emotions; it helps us work out what is most important in our lives. Instead of book reports, let's promote responses that allow and encourage students to explore thoughtfully their likes, dislikes, interests, experiences, and emotional responses. Let's offer reading-response options that encourage rather than discourage reading—options that extend beyond the written format of book reports to include oral and dramatic response, as well as the opportunity for artistic representations of text.

Ban the Book Report presents 20 classroom-tested reading-response assignments, focused on personal response (including emotional response) to independent reading. Some assignments invite students to present an oral or visual response that definitely goes beyond the rigid format of standard written book reports. Each of the 20 assignments is complemented with a rubric in student-friendly language, a completion form, and two exemplars of student responses. Since exemplars show rather than tell what is possible, they powerfully illustrate reading-response possibilities to students.

Detailed literary analysis and instruction in reading skills certainly deserve an honored place in language arts programs. However, the proper location for this emphasis is in the intensive study of selected texts, rather than in extended or free-time reading. While teachers certainly nudge students to read carefully and reflectively in independent reading, the emphasis must be on enjoyment and personal response. When students respond to their independent reading, they comment honestly on their responses and use textual evidence to explain responses.

Encourage students to share reactions similar to the following comments about their favorite books:

> I enjoy reading books that relate to my way of living, books that deal with the problems I have to deal with.

I felt completely involved in the story. The joys, sorrows, and major events were so strong, it seemed to be happening to me.

The story dealt with outdoor life—fishing and hunting. It focused on a young man who loved the outdoors. I especially liked his interest in nature and outdoor activities.

An emphasis on varied personal-response options need not imply a lack of academic challenge or rigor. The 20 response options suggested in this book challenge students to support their responses with specific textual references and reasoning. However, the thinking that students demonstrate connects to their interests and to what is important in their lives. Response options involve higher-level thinking skills, including the evaluation of information, but do so in a way that is motivational to students.

Ban the Book Report begins with a review of why frequent independent reading is important to students and how school programs effectively promote frequent independent reading. The part of the book titled Motivational Reading-Response Assignments presents student-ready assignments, rubrics, completion forms, and exemplars for 20 reading-response options. The book concludes with suggestions for developing motivational reading-response assignments similar to those presented in this book; eight assignments, suggested by teachers, have been included.

The More Reading, the Better

Teachers recognize the benefits of frequent independent reading by students—increased knowledge on a range of topics, enhanced vocabulary, and improved reading comprehension. Instead of narrow and analytical book reports, response assignments should be more closely aligned with the reasons that people read voluntarily: exploring personal interests, making important emotional connections, and enjoying themselves. Teachers who value showing as well as telling expectations appreciate resources that illustrate motivated reading responses and powerful personal connections to one's reading.

1 Meaning that Includes Personal Significance

Response to independent reading must value meaning-making that includes emotional response and personal connections as well as thematic meaning and stylistic analysis.

Reading research has long emphasized the importance of frequent independent reading by students, not only for reading comprehension but also for enrichment of students' lives. For years we have recognized that without encouragement many young people would not voluntarily read longer texts, such as novels. The digital age intensifies the challenge, since online reading is often characterized by skimming, scanning, and shuffling around multiple texts rather than extended reflective reading of longer texts. Despite the challenges, educators must clearly and enthusiastically advocate frequent independent reading. The independent reading habit is a gift that yields lifetime enjoyment and opportunity.

Teachers and parents should remember frequent independent reading leads to writing. Published writers frequently report that their reading led them to their writing and that without their reading habit they never would have become writers. Even if one's writing is never published or even shared with others, it represents a highly significant form of personal exploration and self-understanding.

To encourage students to read frequently and independently, stress the following program features:

- Students enjoy access to a wide collection of reading materials in classroom and school libraries.
- Students have the opportunity to hear books read aloud.
- Students spend class time reading self-selected texts.
- Students talk about and write about their personal and emotional responses.

Critical analysis or personal response—which is more likely to motivate lifelong reading? Since book reports are impersonal and analytical, rather than personal and reflective, offer your students response options other than book reports for independent reading.

The meaning readers create when they read extends beyond thematic meaning, and effective response options recognize this. Of course, readers interpret the themes presented in texts. These themes often confirm or challenge beliefs, and usefully do so. However, meaning also includes emotional understandings and reflection on the readers' personal experiences. When a reader reports being unable to stop reading the book, the reader has emotionally connected to the text. Thinking about why a book is so emotionally appealing represents a truly valuable and motivational exploration of meaning.

Finally, when readers connect the experiences presented in text to their own experiences, when they compare fictional characters, conflicts, motivations, and settings to their own lives or to characters, conflicts, motivations, and settings encountered in other fiction, they engage in a personally meaningful and academically significant exploration. When they compare information, observations, and interpretations presented in nonfiction to their own current understanding, based on personal experience and reading of other texts, once again, readers are engaging in meaningful learning. Response to independent reading must value meaning-making that includes emotional response and personal connections as well as thematic meaning and stylistic analysis.

Conferences and Surveys

Boys often prefer practical how-to and informational texts.

In conferences with students, especially students who claim not to enjoy reading, teachers and librarians can usefully invite students to identify subjects of interest—football, hockey, cars, horses, magazines, movies, and so on. Librarians provide invaluable help in matching reluctant readers with texts linked to their current personal interests. In recommending texts based on current interest, we can encourage students to extend their reading tastes over time. In helping students select texts with an appropriate level of difficulty, we can nudge students toward more challenging and more literary texts as their reading abilities develop. With guidance, a reader can be led by a favorite author, topic, or genre to similar and possibly more challenging books.

Matching students with personally significant and motivational books becomes a major focus as teachers encourage frequent independent reading. When students claim to dislike reading, respond that they just haven't yet discovered the right book and that the right book awaits discovery by every reader. Work from the conviction that there are interesting books for every student, books that motivate personal involvement and lifelong reading, books that lead readers enthusiastically to recommend titles to other students.

See page 15 for a reproducible version of My Current Reading for Pleasure Survey; see page 16 for My Current Reading Profile.

Reading profiles or surveys represent one strategy to guide students in their choices of books for independent reading. Consider using surveys like those on pages 15 and 16 in a class discussion about favorite reading. Have students revisit the survey throughout the school year, so they can note changes in their reading preferences.

My Current Reading for Pleasure Survey

NAME: *Chris Lopez*   DATE: April 25

I like books that are *fictional, romantic and funny.*
I am likely to reread material that is written *by my favorite author or that is fun to read.*
I dislike books that are *always talking about tragic events.*
My favorite place for reading is *in my room.*
I would like to read more about *fictional, romance books.*
I would describe the amount of reading that I do as *a hobby; an enjoyment.*
I am likely to finish a book that *that has a great plot.*
I am unlikely to finish a book that *always talks about bad, depressing stuff.*
For the next month, my personal reading goal is to *re-read the Twilight Series of Stephanie Meyer and try out other books.*

My Current Reading Profile

NAME: *Ann Shaefer*   DATE: September 12

The first part I look at in a novel is *the front picture.*

I like to read novels that look at *something scary or surprising.*

One thing that "puts me off" reading a novel is *when the author says the same thing over and over again.*

I usually read a novel in about *one day* (days, weeks).

My favorite authors are *Peg Kehret.*

When I describe myself as a reader, I usually use phrases such as *fast, good.*

My good reading habits are *I read fast and can summarize a book.*

Reading habits I would like to change are *to stop reading a book in one day or less.*

My personal reading goals for this term (week/month) are *to read something different than chick-flicks and scary books.*

School Library Collections

School library collections strongly influence the viability of independent reading effort. Teachers and librarians must constantly monitor and update classroom and school library holdings, paying particular attention to authors, titles, and subjects that appeal to students. Collections should include graphic novels, texts at a range of reading levels, a range of informational texts, fiction and poetry, and audio books.

Recorded reading or audio books allow students to enjoy texts beyond their reading level. It is critical that students follow the print as the text is read so that they learn print forms of oral language. In some independent reading programs, volunteers record readings of texts or serve as reading buddies; i.e., partners who read the book with the students.

See page 106 for titles that can assist you in maintaining current library sources.

Oral Reading and Book Talks

Many adults identify a teacher's reading aloud as their favorite memory of school—a memory that inspires their own lifelong reading.

Encourage frequent independent reading by regularly sharing your own competent and enthusiastic reading of appealing texts in a variety of literary forms. When students present a competent oral reading of a favorite part of a text, it can motivate other students to read the book.

Follow these guidelines to improve your oral reading of texts. Encourage students to apply these techniques when they engage in oral reading.

- Respect Punctuation Cues: Many readers pause unnaturally in oral reading. Unnatural pauses impair a listener's comprehension of an oral reading. Remember that a comma signals a pause; a period signals a stop. An exclamation mark signals emotion; a question mark signals an inquisitive tone, and, in some cases, a tone of disbelief or anger.
- Use Timing and Pacing: Decide how quickly the text will be read and where changes in pace are appropriate.
- Vary Volume: Different texts require different volume and changes in volume.

- Use Emphasis: Remember that an effective oral reading always moves to a focal point. Choose the point of emphasis. Signal it with a slight pause and a deliberate emphasis of key words.

Good Bits conferences represent another possibility to encourage students to read extensively. A *good bit* is a part of a text that the reader finds interesting, enjoyable, memorable, or personally important. Following your modeling of a Good Bit conference, students take turns sharing good bits with the entire class or a group of classmates. Provide them with these guidelines:

- Provide a little background about the text and why you chose it.
- Read the good bit as effectively as you can.
- Tell why you like the good bit, why it is enjoyable for you.
- Invite questions and reactions from others.

Reading Targets and Contests

A school's independent reading program sometimes includes the setting of targets—often a minimum of five to ten books per year. The targets specify dates that reading responses are due. Ideally, students will voluntarily read beyond the minimum targets.

Each personal-response assignment in this book includes the requirement that students report on reading completed; e.g., the entire book.

Each personal-response assignment in this book includes the requirement that students report on reading completed; e.g., the entire book, at least half of the book, less than half of the book, little or none of the book. Consider whether students will complete responses for books that they have not read entirely. If they have not completely read the book by the date on which a response is due, you might challenge them to do so by the next due date. You might suggest that students complete a response based on a partial reading of the text and then move on to another book that might be more motivational. As a feature of differentiated instruction, set different reading targets for different students.

It is a good idea to provide a reading folder for each student. The folder will contain reading surveys completed by the students throughout the year, as well as the students responses to independent reading. A few times during the year, challenge students to review the collection to select what they think is their best response, with a page attached to explain their choice. Encourage students to identify a personal reading goal as part of the assessment. With their own and parents' permission, students share responses in classroom displays and presentations. Such sharing motivates other students to read the book and illustrates possibilities for thoughtful reading responses.

Selection criteria for best responses should be negotiated in class.

Be wary of contests as part of independent reading programs. Schools that employ prizes, such as pizza, hockey cards, and merchandise, suggest that reading is a chore that is good for you but requires an extrinsic reward. While contests and prizes might motivate students to develop a love of reading, often the reading ends at the end of the contest. Instead, emphasize that reading is enjoyable and personally important; therefore, reading is its own reward and often is a better entertainment option than a prize item.

Timed Reading Records

To promote independent readers, allow class time for independent reading, expecting that reading time will be used productively. Many teachers employ timed reading periods and records to encourage focused and productive reading. They report that students' reading rate and comprehension improve as a result. Key features of timed reading include the following:

- Students complete a separate form for each book that they are reading. This form is kept in a folder.
- Before the reading period, students record the date and the page on which they begin their reading. They may use estimates, such as "top of page 5."
- Use a timer for a set reading period, often 15 to 20 minutes. When the timer sounds at the end of the period, students stop reading.
- Students record the page on which they stopped reading. In addition, they calculate the number of pages they have read and add a brief comment, summary, or prediction.

Independent Reading Record
Name: *Kim Tan*
Title of Text: *Tom Sawyer*

Date	Start Page	Finish Page	Pages Read	Comment
Oct. 5	*15 (top)*	*20 (middle)*	*4 ½*	*The part about Tom giving medicine to the cat is funny. I wonder if this could happen in real life.*

Celebrations of Reading

A school's independent reading program will be enhanced when celebrations are included. Celebrations remind students that reading enhances one's life. In the spirit of celebration, speakers talk about why reading is important to them, their favorite reading, and their favorite memories of reading. Sometimes they will present a competent oral reading from a favorite book.

In inviting speakers to talk about their favorite reading, offer suggestions such as the following:

- My favorite children's book
- The book I liked best when I was a child
- A book that made me believe in myself
- My favorite book about an inspirational person
- Books that helped me become a writer
- A book I couldn't stop reading
- A book that inspired me to travel
- My favorite adventure book
- My favorite fantasy or science fiction book
- My favorite book of poetry
- A favorite story that someone told me
- A book that helped me deal with loneliness

Special events for reading celebrations might feature authors, community members, and students. Events can be planned for classrooms or larger venues.

- A book that made me understand that it's okay to be different
- My favorite book about being a friend
- A book that made me more considerate of others
- A book that helped me overcome a prejudice
- My favorite picture book
- A book that helped me complete a project
- A book that helped me learn something new
- A book that helped me learn something important about the world
- A book that helped me choose my career

Following a speaker's talk about one or more of these topics, engage students in discussion about their favorite reading. What recommendations would students make about their favorite children's books, adventure books, poetry books, informational books? What books helped them believe in themselves and become more compassionate? If a student was stranded on a deserted island with only one book, which book would it be?

Using Rubrics and Exemplars

Each assignment in this book contains a rubric written in student-friendly language. These rubrics highlight key features of the response task. Teachers are encouraged to add, delete, and modify the criteria in the rubrics.

In addition, each assignment includes two student-written exemplars. While rubrics tell about expectations, exemplars show expectations as well as possibilities. Through exemplars, you can demonstrate features that make a response useful and interesting to other readers. In many classrooms, teachers post exemplars to emphasize their usefulness to students. They report immense motivational benefit in the use of exemplars. Typically, the quality of individual responses improves over time as students incorporate features of the exemplars in their own responses.

Notes on each of the 20 assignments can guide you in your recommendations to students.

Recommend reading-response assignments that you judge to be motivational and appropriate for students. Which assignments will students find interesting? Which will encourage honest personal response, including emotional response? Which assignments are the most natural fit for the book the student has read? You might assign one selected assignment or allow a measure of student choice. Most teachers who have worked with the material offer two or three choices at a time. With this approach, students focus on the exemplars in a manageable way.

Once assignments have been selected, students review and discuss the exemplars to learn about possibilities and expectations. If they need additional learning, they might engage in more-detailed study of the exemplars. Students work actively with the two exemplars related to the selected assignment and, with your guidance, complete one of these learning activities:

1. From the set of two exemplars, identify the more proficient response and explain your choice.
2. Employ the rubric to assess the two exemplars.
3. Suggest details to add, delete, or modify to improve the exemplars.
4. Considering specific criteria from the rubric, use sticky notes or highlighters to mark strengths in the exemplar.

Following their work with the related exemplars, students complete their reading-response assignments. Before submitting their assignments to the teacher, they use the rubric to assess their own work. Sometimes students will work with peers as they employ the rubric to suggest revisions to others' reading responses. Each rubric challenges students to identify what they like best about their responses and to identify a goal for next time. Teachers use the same rubric to assess student work.

My Current Reading for Pleasure Survey

NAME: DATE:

I like books that are

I am likely to reread material that is

I dislike books that are

My favorite place for reading is

I would like to read more about

I would describe the amount of reading that I do as

I am likely to finish a book that

I am unlikely to finish a book that

Pembroke Publishers © 2012 *Ban the Book Report* by Graham Foster ISBN 978-1-55138-264-7

My Current Reading Profile

NAME: DATE:

The first part I look at in a novel is

I like to read novels that look at

One thing that "puts me off" reading a novel is

I usually read a novel in about _____ (days, weeks)
My favorite authors are

When I describe myself as a reader, I usually use phrases such as

My good reading habits are

Reading habits I would like to change are

My personal reading goals for this term (week/month) are

Pembroke Publishers © 2012 *Ban the Book Report* by Graham Foster ISBN 978-1-55138-264-7

Motivational Reading-Response Assignments

Assignments have been designed for response to both fiction and nonfiction, and are planned to encourage personal response, including emotional response to text and the opportunity for students to consider items of personal interest. In addition, the assignments challenge close and thoughtful reading of text.

This collection of reading response assignments has been organized into the following chapters:

2 Reading Log Assignments

This section includes three assignments: Reading Log Prompts, Reading Log Prompts Focusing on Conflict, and Reading Log at Key Points During Reading.

Reading Log Prompts challenge students to complete six brief statements to questions about their reading experience and their personal response. Teachers report that this assignment works well early in the school year. Students who do better with short assignment segments prefer the specific focus of each of the six questions to longer, more open-ended tasks.

Reading Log Prompts Focusing on Conflict work well with fiction in which a character's conflicts are a critical focus. The assignment particularly benefits students for whom the goal of thinking carefully about conflict and the consequences of a character's choice is an appropriate instructional focus. Teachers report that this assignment is a popular student choice, especially for students who work better with short assignments.

Reading Log at Key Points During Reading challenges students to pause and note reactions twice during their reading of a book, as well as to record their thoughts once they have finished reading the book. Students find this assignment more challenging than the other two reading-log options. This assignment is more open-ended, and therefore appeals to students who can handle a measure of choice. Teachers recommend this assignment to students who would benefit from slowing down to be more reflective during their reading of a book.

Reading Log Prompts

Write a paragraph for each prompt. Present specific information that will help your reader decide whether or not to read the book. Focus on providing important details and reasons for your response and on writing clearly and correctly. Remember that your reader has probably not read the book. Supply any background information that your reader needs.

1. Would you read another book by this author? Why or why not?
2. What part of the book did you enjoy the most?
3. What part of the book surprised you the most?
4. What did the book prompt you to think about or consider?
5. What other books are like this one?
6. What questions does this book raise for you? Why?

Name: _____   Date: _____

	I'm not there yet	I'm getting there	I'm there now
Information about the Book	My response lacks specific information about the book. My reader will not have enough information to decide about reading it.	My response presents some information about the book. However, my reader will need additional information to decide about reading it.	My response presents enough information about the book to help my reader decide about reading it.
Reasoning	I need to add details and reasons to my response.	I include adequate details and reasons in my response.	I present extensive details and reasons in my response.
Presentation	My word choice is imprecise. I am careless with spelling and grammar/usage.	My word choice is accurate. A few mistakes with spelling and grammar/usage distract my reader.	My word choice is precise and effective. I have few or no mistakes in spelling and grammar/usage.

Reading Completed

Book Title: _____   Author: _____

❑ I have read the entire book.
❑ I have read at least half of the book.
❑ I have read less than half of the book.
❑ I have read little or none of the book.

What I like best about my response: _____

_____

My reading goal for my next book: _____

_____

Pembroke Publishers © 2012 *Ban the Book Report* by Graham Foster ISBN 978-1-55138-264-7

Reading Log Prompts

Book Title: *A Series of Unfortunate Events: The Miserable Mill*   Author: Lemony Snicket

1. Would you read another book by this author? Why or why not?

The book I read was very fun and exciting. I love this author and his books. The next book I read will definitely be by this author, Lemony Snicket. I like to read books by this author because he is a good author and writes books that leave cliff-hangers so you always want to read more. I'm looking forward to reading another one of his amazing books.

2. What part of the book did you enjoy the most?

I loved to read this book: I had a lot of favorite parts I liked, but the one I most enjoyed was the part when the big fight happened near the end with Sunny fighting Dr. Orwell, and Violet and Foreman Flacutono. In addition, Klaus had to save Charles from being sliced in half by a giant saw just as he came out of hypnosis. This was my favorite part because it was very exciting and I couldn't stop reading.

3. What part of the book surprised you the most?

This book had lots of surprises, but the thing that surprised me the most was that Foreman Flaucutono was Count Olaf's assistant. I was not thinking that Foreman was Olaf's assistant. I thought he was Count Olaf.

4. What did the book prompt you to think about or consider?

The book made me question and think about a lot as I kept reading. I mostly thought about the children (Baudelaires). I felt so sorry for them knowing that they had been through so much. I wonder how they would feel and what they were going through. Their talents also made me think a lot. They have amazing talents and they are so smart. You could say that they weren't ordinary kids.

5. What other books are like this one?

There are many books like the one I read. The book I read was the fourth in the series of thirteen. For what I know there are twelve other books that are the same as this one. With Violet, Klaus and Sunny always having unlucky luck and with Count Olaf's trying to steal their fortune. All of the books are also by the same author, Lemony Snicket.

6. What questions does this book raise for you? Why?

As I read and read this book, so many things were going through my head. I have many questions about this book. One of them was why was Count Olaf so mean and what made him want to do all of his evil deeds. I'm questioning this because in the book Count Olaf wants to steal the Baudelaire fortune but there was nothing saying why he wanted to or what does he need the money for. His motive is one of the questions I had when I was reading.

Pembroke Publishers © 2012 *Ban the Book Report* by Graham Foster ISBN 978-1-55138-264-7

Reading Log Prompts

Book Title: *The One Left Behind*   Author: S.A. Bodeen

1. Would you read another book by this author? Why or why not?
I would most definitely read another book by this author because I had never heard of this author before and I couldn't set the book down until I was done and I read it again in four days. So I'm hoping if I read another one of the books it would be just as intriguing.

2. What part of the book did you enjoy the most?
I enjoyed the ending most because it was the scariest I've read and every page presented a new mystery that would occur or unfold. It was amazing because I never have got scared of books before but this one wouldn't let me sleep at night after I had finished.

3. What part of the book surprised you the most?
The part that really shocked me was when Mandy explained to the readers how her twin died from eating bad meat. I wasn't expecting that would be the reason she died because the feeling of the book made it seem that it would be a mystery how she died.

4. What parts did the book prompt you to think about or consider?
The one part that really made me think was when Mandy went downstairs and the doors were unlocked, the window was open, the TV was on and there was no food missing because she had locked the windows and doors and the town she lived in was crime free.

5. What other books are like this one?
I can't really think of a book that was like this one because it was so different but I would say that S.A. Bodeen's books are similar. Her book THE COMPOUND has a similar theme to it.

6. What questions does this book raise for you? Why?
The end made it seem like the author would write a second book because it was such a cliffhanger. It would make me ask questions like "Are Zander and Dusty okay?" "Did Mandy get over Angle's death?" I also think she left a lot of cliffhangers in the middle and beginning or the book as well because everything always seemed like a mystery.

Pembroke Publishers © 2012 *Ban the Book Report* by Graham Foster ISBN 978-1-55138-264-7

Reading Log Prompts Focusing on Conflict

Write a paragraph for each prompt. Present specific information about the conflict in your book. Remember that your reader may not have read the book. Focus on showing how difficult the choices are. For the final prompt, provide reasons to explain your judgment about whether the character made effective choices.

1. What conflict or conflicts did the central character deal with?
2. What choices does the character make to deal with conflict or conflicts?
3. What are the consequences of the character's choices to deal with conflict or conflicts?
4. Do you think that the character makes effective choices to deal with conflict? If not, what better choices could the character have made?

Name: _____   Date: _____

	I'm not there yet	I'm getting there	I'm there now
Information about the Book	My response does not help my reader understand difficulties faced by the main character in dealing with conflicts.	My response helps my reader understand difficulties faced by the main character but I could add detail to explain the conflicts.	My response clearly and adequately explains difficulties faced by the main character in dealing with the conflict.
Reasoning	I need to add information to explain whether my character makes effective choices.	I present adequate information to explain whether my character makes effective choices.	I present extensive information to explain whether my character makes effective choices.
Presentation	My response could be more clearly worded. I am careless with spelling and grammar/usage.	My response is clearly worded. A few mistakes with grammar/usage distract my reader.	My response is effectively worded. I have few or no mistakes in spelling or grammar/usage.

Reading Completed

Book Title: _____   Author: _____

❑ I have read the entire book.
❑ I have read at least half of the book.
❑ I have read less than half of the book.
❑ I have read little or none of the book.

What I like best about my response: _____

_____

My reading goal for my next book: _____

_____

Pembroke Publishers © 2012 *Ban the Book Report* by Graham Foster ISBN 978-1-55138-264-7

Reading Log Prompts Focusing on Conflict

Book Title: *The Lightning Thief*   Author: Rick Riordan

1. What conflict or conflicts did the central character deal with?
The conflict that the central character dealt with occurred when Percy Jackson was being accused of stealing Zeus' master bolt because he was the son of Poseidon. If Percy couldn't return the master bolt in exactly ten days, a war amongst the gods would begin. To succeed on his quest, he must not only catch the real thief of the bolt but also understand what the Oracle had said to him. He must also succeed in saving his mother from the dog of the underworld, Hades.

2. What choices does the character make to deal with conflict or conflicts?
A choice Percy had to make was to choose between staying safe in Camp Half-Blood or embarking into the dangerous world and retrieving the master bolt. He chose to retrieve the master bolt. Another choice he had to make was when he met Ares, he either had to trust him or leave Ares alone and not help him.

3. What were the consequences of the character's choices to deal with conflict or conflicts?
The consequences of retrieving the master bolt resulted in his having to go to the underworld and confront Hades, having to fight Medusa and having to fight several monsters who were disguised as humans. The consequences of trusting Ares resulted in Percy's almost being killed in an abandoned water park and being betrayed by Ares after he had done him a good deed.

4. Do you think that the character made effective choices to deal with conflict? If not, what better choices could the character have made?
I believe that Percy made some effective choices and some not so effective choices. Returning the master bolt was an effective choice because he stopped a major war from occurring. A not so effective choice he made was trusting the god of war, Ares. The god of war desired conflict among the gods but Percy wasn't smart enough to see this.

Pembroke Publishers © 2012 *Ban the Book Report* by Graham Foster ISBN 978-1-55138-264-7

Reading Log Prompts Focusing on Conflict

Book Title: *Shield of Stars*   Author: Hilari Bell

1. What conflict or conflicts did the central character deal with?
The SHIELD OF STARS follows the former pick-pocket, Weasel, who now serves as a law clerk for Justice Holis in a land called Deothas. Justice Holis is later charged with treason against the tyrannical regent Pettibone (yes, Pettibone), a crime that Justice Holis and many others are, in fact, guilty of. As such, it's up to Weasel, the law clerk, to pick up his old pick-pocket skills and bust Justice Holis out of jail. Only problem is that he only has two weeks to do it!

2. What choices does the character make to deal with conflict or conflicts?
At first Weasel tries to free Holis by having the downtrodden Prince Edoran release Holis, a ploy that does not work. What a shocker! Weasel ends up getting thrown in jail. Actually, he's only held in a modified supply room, where he meets a tomboy, country girl with combat skills, a girl named Arisa. (Okay, she's only a slight tomboy.) Together they escape. After they escape, Weasel decides to find the road bandit, revolutionary Falcon. Arisa agrees to help him.

3. What were the consequences of the character's choices to deal with the conflict or conflicts?
Weasel and Arisa first try to reach the Falcon by contacting a banned religion but this doesn't work, so they then try to contact the Falcon through the criminal underground. This scheme ends with Arisa's getting kidnapped. After a brief interlude, Weasel rescues Arisa from her kidnappers. She then reveals that not only is the Falcon a woman but that Arisa is her daughter. What a surprise! Arisa takes Weasel to the Falcon's camp and after a good night's sleep, they plan a prison breakout. After arriving at the capital city and breaking and entering the castle, Weasel finds a really important shield that easily gives someone political advantage. After abusing this advantage, the Falcon shoots Prince Pettibone through the head effectively killing him! Justice Holis is released and they start the rehabilitation of Deothas.

4. Do you think the character made effective choices? If not, what better choices could the character make?
Weasel probably could have made better choices. For instance, he could have trusted his criminal instincts and not his law clerk's brain. Despite this, it was a really good book that anyone could read. And you should read it too, so go read it right now!

Pembroke Publishers © 2012 *Ban the Book Report* by Graham Foster ISBN 978-1-55138-264-7

Reading Log at Key Points During Reading

As you read your book, pause twice to record your thoughts. In addition, record your thoughts once you have finished reading the book. Comment on some of the following:

- predictions
- questions
- likes
- personal connections

- points of uncertainty
- developing understanding
- dislikes
- favorite parts

In your final entry, comment on the accuracy of predictions, answers to questions, what you came to understand, what you changed your mind about, and how your likes and dislikes changed or did not change.

Name: _____   Date: _____

	I'm not there yet	I'm getting there	I'm there now
Information about the Book	My reading log entries present little or no detail about my thoughts and reactions as I read the book.	My reading log entries present adequate detail about my thoughts and reactions as I read the book.	My reading log entries present thorough detail about my thoughts and reactions as I read the book.
Reasoning	My reading log entries do not include reasons for my thoughts and reactions.	My reading log entries include reasons for my thoughts and reactions.	My reading log entries include detailed reasons for my thoughts and reactions.
Presentation	My word choice is imprecise. I am careless with spelling and grammar/usage.	My word choice is clear. A few mistakes in spelling and grammar/usage distract my reader.	My word choice is precise and effective. I have few or no mistakes in spelling and grammar/usage.

Reading Completed

Book Title: _____   Author: _____

- ❏ I have read the entire book.
- ❏ I have read at least half of the book.
- ❏ I have read less than half of the book.
- ❏ I have read little or none of the book.

What I like best about my response: _____

_____

My reading goal for my next book: _____

_____

Pembroke Publishers © 2012 *Ban the Book Report* by Graham Foster ISBN 978-1-55138-264-7

Reading Log at Key Points During Reading

Book Title: *Holes*   Author: Louis Sachar

Pause 1: *Chapters 1–16*

At the very beginning of HOLES by Louis Sachar, Stanley, the son of an unknown inventor, finds a famous baseball player's shoes. Stanley is then punished for stealing the shoes—a crime he didn't commit. After going to court, Stanley gets a choice to either go to jail or go to Camp Green Lake. I was surprised at this because generally in our court system, you don't get a choice in your sentence. One of the biggest shockers in this book was that Camp Green Lake wasn't even a lake. It was a dried up lake with lots of holes. I thought that it was going to be one continuous story but then I realized in Chapter 7 that it actually told the story of Camp Green Lake through the eyes of Stanley's great-great grandfather, Elya Yelnats. Now, I understood that Stanley's relative is very important to the story. My favorite part in Chapters 1–16 would have to be learning about Camp Green Lake.

Pause 2: *Chapters 17–32*

After learning about the history of Camp Green Lake, I was more interested in what would happen when I got nearer to the ending. In these chapters the reader learns that in fact there are two main characters, Hector "Zero" Zeroni and Stanley Yelnats I (Caveman). After I read these chapters, I was surprised with the nicknames given to the two main characters from the fellow occupants at Camp Green Lake. When I learned this, I was surprised that the author named them after their vivid character descriptions. After one event in Chapter 17, I finally put two and two together and realized that the occupants of Camp Green Lake weren't digging to build character but to find treasure. I found this out by the flashback to Elya's life. My favorite part of this chapter is when Stanley stole the sunflowers and got in trouble with Mr. Pendanski. What surprised me in this part is when the Warden got upset with Mr. Sir for disturbing her for nothing.

Book Completed: *Chapters 33–50*

After Stanley stole the sunflower seeds, Zero ran away. Then Stanley ran away. At that moment, I thought that Stanley and Zero would never meet up and waste away to nothing. My favorite part in the ending of the book is when Stanley's father (the scientist) discovered a new way of recycling sneakers and pays bail for Stanley. I was questioning the ending because I thought it would be a disappointing ending but it wasn't.

Pembroke Publishers © 2012 *Ban the Book Report* by Graham Foster ISBN 978-1-55138-264-7

Reading Log at Key Points During Reading

Book Title: *The Sun of Neptune*   Author: Rick Riordan

Pause 1: *Chapters 1–14*

At this point in THE SUN OF NEPTUNE I predict that eventually Percy, Frank and Hazel will have to embark on some sort of journey—most possibly a quest. I expect that Percy will meet up with the people from Camp Half-Blood. One question for the author that I have is, "Why does Nico diAngelo travel so much?" I like Rick Riordan's sense of humor and how he includes all the background information that took place before the book started. I dislike that at times it seems obvious what will happen, such as Frank telling Percy to blow up the water cannons. One point of uncertainty I had as a I read was when a character named Don the faun was introduced, because he acted differently from other satyrs. I am developing an understanding of why Frank's life depended on a piece of wood when the back story started. At first, I was very confused, but the story is gradually explaining different parts. I felt sympathy for Hazel when I discovered that she was dead. My favorite part so far is when Percy and Hazel walk in when Octavian is gutting those stuffed animals.

Pause 2: *Chapter 15–29*

Right now, I predict that something horrible will happen to Frank. I predict this because at the R.O.F.L. store, Iris stated "The task ahead of you....Well, I wouldn't wish it on anyone, especially a nice boy like you." A question I have for the author is "Why does Gaea want Percy to go to Alaska?" I think that that will probably be revealed in time. I like how Gaea is really malevolent, evil and all-knowing. Readers get a sense of her character by the way the author describes her. I dislike Frank's character out of all the main characters. I think that he is timid, but his character seems to be improving. A point of uncertainty I have occurred when Hazel shares details of her blackout with Frank. My favorite part is when Percy talks about the man Satchel and then threatens the whale. That was very humorous.

Book Complete: *Chapter 30 to end*

I predicted that Percy and his quest party will kill again and free Thanatos. I predicted this because that fact is becoming obvious with Percy's dream and other facts. I like how the characters developed throughout the book and how their bond strengthened. I developed an understanding of Juno's motives. My favorite part at the end of the book was in Alaska when they were observing the Hyperborean giants. The precise description and action kept me reading. I highly recommend this book because of the page-turning plot but most of all because of Rick Riordan's sense of humor.

Pembroke Publishers © 2012 *Ban the Book Report* by Graham Foster ISBN 978-1-55138-264-7

3   Oral Response Assignments

Chapter 8 includes two other oral response assignments: Create and Perform a Dramatic Script (page 101) and Readers' Theatre (page 102).

This section presents four possibilities: Book Talk for Fiction, Oral Reading of My Favorite Part of the Book, Reading Surprises, and Talk Show Interview.

Book Talk for Fiction works well for students who need to develop confidence with their oral language. The assignments present specific and manageable segments that help students organize their book talks.

Oral Reading of My Favorite Part of the Book benefits students who lack confidence in oral reading. Rather than stressful round-robin reading, this assignment allows students to prepare and practice their reading carefully before they present it to the class. Teachers who assign this task two or three times throughout the school year report significant improvement in the second and third attempts. Most students have little difficulty with the open-ended personal response statement that concludes the reading.

Reading Surprises can be completed as a written assignment or an oral presentation. Even though students often enjoy books with surprising twists, they sometimes struggle with interpreting the meaning of the surprise. Without doubt, this assignment is more challenging than the previous two in the section. The assignment is recommended for students who can handle a challenge.

Talk-Show Interview can also be completed as a written assignment or an oral presentation. Obviously, in an oral presentation, the student needs to work with a partner to present the interview to the class. This assignment is a popular choice among students. They appreciate the conversational approach of the talk-show interview. Most students prefer the written assignment to the oral presentation.

Book Talk for Fiction

Present a brief talk about your book to comment on the items below. Be sure to provide detailed information that will help your reader decide about the book. Remember that your audience probably contains people who have not read it. For items 3 and 4, provide reasons for your response. Speak clearly and emphatically.

1. What is the work of fiction about?
2. What major conflicts does the central character face?
3. Which character do you find most interesting? Why?
4. Identify readers who might enjoy the text. Why would it appeal to them?

Name: _____   Date: _____

	I'm not there yet	I'm getting there	I'm there now
Information about the Book	My response lacks specific information about the book. My listener will not have enough information to decide about reading it.	My response includes some information about the book. However, my listener will need additional information to decide about reading it.	My response includes enough detailed information about the book to help my listener decide about reading it.
Reasoning	I need to add reasons to explain my response.	I include adequate reasons for my response.	I present extensive reasons for my response.
Presentation	I need to speak more clearly with more effective pace and volume.	I have one specific challenge: to improve the clarity, pace, or volume in my speaking.	I consistently speak clearly, with appropriate pace and adequate volume.

Reading Completed

Book Title: _____   Author: _____

❑ I have read the entire book.
❑ I have read at least half of the book.
❑ I have read less than half of the book.
❑ I have read little or none of the book.

What I like best about my response: _____

_____

My reading goal for my next book: _____

_____

Pembroke Publishers © 2012 *Ban the Book Report* by Graham Foster ISBN 978-1-55138-264-7

Book Talk for Fiction

Book Title: *Lockdown: Escape from Furnace*   Author: Alexander Gordon Smith

The story is about Alex Sawyer, a young criminal, and his journey to hell and back. He was framed for his best friend's death. He was sentenced to a place that people believed was worse than hell—Furnace Penitentiary, where monsters kill you in the middle of the night and where people just don't care whether you die or not. Obviously, Alex couldn't handle the place. He had to escape. He had to. Alex recruited two cellmates whom he had met and they found an underground river that they believe led to an escape. But on the night before the scheduled escape, one of his helpers was taken in the dead of the night by the creatures who ruled Furnace. This greatly affected the plan that Alex had worked on for a long while. The plan must go on. He was able to leave with his other cellmate but ended up getting badly hurt. They had left hell……for now.

Alex faced various conflicts. He faced getting caught during a heist and having his best friend killed right before his eyes. Then he had to face another friend being killed before his eyes. He almost danced with death a few times. In addition, rabid dogs that ate human flesh chased him around the penitentiary. Gang members almost beat him to death and he was almost pierced to death by jagged rocks.

I found that Donovan, Alex's escape partner, was a very interesting character. He had to act tough at Furnace but was actually a very kind-hearted kid. He had killed his mother's boyfriend for his mother's own protection. Even when he was threatened with death, he protected Alex. He had a tough shell but was soft on the inside.

People who like very descriptive, suspenseful books should be very interested in this book. It is very suspenseful and has a great amount of description to boot.

Book Talk for Fiction

Book Title: *Death Benefits*   Author: Sarah N. Harvey

This work of fiction is about a young man named Royce. He recently has gone through some major changes. His mom has dragged him across the country so that they could live closer to his grandpa. The grandfather, Arthur, is a famous retired cello player. Unfortunately, he is a very grumpy man who watches TV, eats ice cream, drinks coffee and sleeps all day. When Royce's mom doesn't know what to do with Arthur, Royce volunteers to take care of him for pay. Royce faces major conflicts everyday dealing with Arthur. He gets Arthur coffee, ice cream and deals with Arthur's grumpy attitude. Royce also faces conflict with himself—his shyness. He meets a girl and he is unsure about how to express his feelings. In addition, Grandpa has a stroke. In fact, Arthur has several strokes and Royce must help him cope. They come to write a book about the famous cello player. These are a few of the conflicts Royce faces.

The character that I found most interesting was Arthur because he was a very complex man. Most days he would be grumpy and angry. Then he would burst out into laughter at random. Arthur was sometimes generous, but he forced it. He appreciated everything Royce and his mother gave him even though he couldn't admit it. Arthur was not as unattractive as others thought.

I think this book would be enjoyable to people who are interested in believable relationships. Readers who are dealing with a similar situation or have people in their lives who are grumpy would probably enjoy the book. It might appeal to them if they want to see how another person of possibly the same age deals with the situation.

Oral Reading of My Favorite Part of the Book

Present an effective oral reading of your favorite part of your book. Provide specific reasons about why you find the part appealing. Invite and respond to comments and questions.

1. What is your favorite part of the book? Read a half page to a full page to your classmates.
2. Why do you like this part of the book?
3. Ask classmates, "Do you have questions or comments?" Respond clearly.

Name: _____   Date: _____

	I'm not there yet	I'm getting there	I'm there now
Information about the Book	I do not offer enough information in response to questions and comments.	I offer some information in response to questions and comments but could be more complete.	My comments and responses to questions provide clear and specific information.
Reasoning	My response lacks clarity and adequate reasoning.	I include adequate reasoning but could add clarity and detail.	I present clear and thorough reasoning for my response.
Presentation	My oral reading is not clear and lacks appropriate pace and volume.	I have one specific challenge: to improve the clarity, pace, or volume of my reading.	My oral reading is clear with appropriate pace and volume.

Reading Completed

Book Title: _____   Author: _____

❑ I have read the entire book.
❑ I have read at least half of the book.
❑ I have read less than half of the book.
❑ I have read little or none of the book.

What I like best about my response: _____

_____

My goal for reading and speaking about my next book: _____

_____

Pembroke Publishers © 2012 *Ban the Book Report* by Graham Foster ISBN 978-1-55138-264-7

Oral Reading of My Favorite Part of the Book

Book Title: *Sylvester and the Magic Pebble*   Author: William Steig

Comments Before Reading My Favorite Part

SYLVESTER AND THE MAGIC PEBBLE is a picture book. Sylvester is a donkey who collects unusual pebbles. One of these pebbles grants him wishes. I don't want to give away too much but I'll tell you that Sylvester makes an unfortunate choice.

Comments Following Sharing of Excerpt

My favorite part of the story is when Sylvester was turned into a rock because it's interesting how out of the blue he wished to be a rock when there was a tiger threatening him. Instead, he could've wished to go back home. But then there would have been no story!

I like this part of the book because I wonder if he was hungry and thirsty. I wonder if he truly wanted to be a rock instead of a donkey. I like it because I like stories that have sad problems. I felt so sorry for Sylvester because I wonder if he's going to turn back to a donkey so he can reunite with his parents again. This part is very interesting because I really want to know what happens next. I also wonder if Sylvester was cold in the winter. Did he stay as a rock forever? This part of the story gave me hope because I knew that Sylvester will turn back to a donkey someday. In addition, this part was a bit funny because I like how he stayed at the same place where he just talked to himself when he should know nobody can hear him and that no one is around him. I felt really sorry for him because it's sad how he had no arms to pick up the red pebble so he can wish to go back to his normal self. I wish I were there to help him so he won't have to feel hopeless and helpless.

Oral Reading of My Favorite Part of the Book

Book Title: *Room*   Author: Emma Donoghue

Comments Before Reading My Favorite Part

ROOM is a book written though the perspective of a 5 year old boy named Jack who was born into life as a captive. His mother was kidnapped as a student in college and has been locked up in a shed in a man's back yard ever since. His only connection to the outside world is through TV, which his mother has told him is all fake. TV helps him to stay contented with his restricted life.

I will read the introduction, where he is just talking about what happens in his typical day and he explains all of the parts of Room.

Comments Following Sharing of Excerpt

I liked this part of the book because I felt it really represented how Room was his equivalent to the World. At first, I thought that there were a lot of grammatical errors, but then I realized that Jack didn't think of objects as objects. In his world, the table was named Table and she had her own traits. The way that Jack had developed personalities for all of the objects in the shed, which he called Room, helped to show me how different life would be if you were always in the same small place. If I were in his mother's shoes, I don't know what I would do. I would want to tell him of the world outside. I'm not sure I'd be able to because if he knew about the world outside, he couldn't tolerate staying in Room. I also believe that this story could be a metaphor for mankind: we feel like we know almost everything about our World, but new discoveries could completely change our perspective at any time.

Pembroke Publishers © 2012 *Ban the Book Report* by Graham Foster ISBN 978-1-55138-264-7

Reading Surprises

In a brief talk or a few paragraphs, identify what surprised you most about your book. Provide reasons for your surprise and about what the surprise helped you understand. Remember that your readers or audience may not have read the book. Be sure to provide them with the background information they need to understand the surprising content that you have selected.

1. Why is this part of the book surprising?
2. What did the surprise help you understand?

Name: _____   Date: _____

	I'm not there yet	I'm getting there	I'm there now
Information about the Book	I provide little information about surprises in the book and what I learned from the surprises.	I identify what surprised me and what I've come to understand but could provide a little more detail.	I clearly identify what surprised me and what I came to understand from surprises in the book.
Reasoning	I offer little background information and detail about why the book surprised me.	I provide adequate background information and detail about why the book surprised me.	I include required background information and thoroughly explain why the book surprised me.
Presentation	My oral or written presentation lacks clarity and organization.	My oral or written presentation is clear and organized.	My oral or written presentation is effective and well-organized.

Reading Completed

Book Title: _____   Author: _____

☐ I have read the entire book.
☐ I have read at least half of the book.
☐ I have read less than half of the book.
☐ I have read little or none of the book.

What I like best about my oral or written presentation: _____

_____

My reading goal for my next book: _____

_____

Pembroke Publishers © 2012 *Ban the Book Report* by Graham Foster ISBN 978-1-55138-264-7

Reading Surprises

Book Title: *The Headless Cupid*   Author: Zilpha Keatley Snyder

Notes to the Author about Surprises in THE HEADLESS CUPID:

I'm a twelve year old with a very busy life but if I'm up to it, I will find myself some time to read, especially if I like the book. I liked the book you wrote. It was fully of mystery, and I love mystery. I really enjoyed reading your book. I didn't waste a minute when it was time for reading because I wanted to find out who the protagonist was. I couldn't figure out whether it was the two girls or the man.

The part of THE HEADLESS CUPID that surprised me most was when Amanda was pretending to be the old ghost of the Westerly place. I mean all those times Amanda's mom and her mom's husband's kids were scared to death and there was nothing to be afraid of because Amanda was the "ghost." I realized that Amanda pretended to be the ghost to convince her family to move out of their house. Amanda preferred living with her father rather than her mother.

It surprised me when Blair and David saw Amanda playing a prank and they decided not to tell anybody they knew because they had just got on Amanda's good side and they didn't want to ruin it.

The séance surprised me because in my mind it was so vivid and real, but I was also surprised that a 12-year-old girl could keep a secret for such a long time.

The surprises helped me understand that it isn't funny but it is mean to play hurtful jokes on someone. I don't think it was right for Amanda to do the ghost stunt because she broke some of her mom's and other people's valuable items, like a vase. It helped me because I learned that what Amanda did was wrong because she really scared people and if I ever do anything close to what Amanda did, there would be big consequences.

You did a really good job writing this book and I would definitely recommend the book to some of my classmates. I like how the book was very detailed in the beginning and got easier at the end. Next time I recommend you get to the problem a little faster, but I guess you wanted the reader to know what Amanda's interests were so it would make more sense.

Reading Surprises

Book Title: *The Dark is Rising*   Author: Susan Cooper

Surprises do not faze me as often as I would like to think, but an exception can definitely be made concerning my time reading THE DARK IS RISING. When I first began reading it, I was more or less expecting a typical fantasy novel; however, it was much more than that. Not only was the story compelling and the suspense phenomenal, but the shocks that were contained within the pages was more than enough to pull me much deeper into the story and make it one of my favorite novels of all time.

One of the first surprises that truly stunned me occurred when Will, the protagonist, ventured down the Oldway Lane, also know more commonly as the Tramps Alley. While traveling down this path, he encountered Maggie Barnes in the unnatural darkness that surrounded the path. Maggie was known to Will's brother, Max. Their conversation started out innocently enough, but then Maggie began acting rather strangely. Her tone darkened and in instances her voice lashed out violently, stating that she "wanted It back"; then she sounded happy and cheerful once more. It soon became apparent that she wanted the signs, two of six important circular objects made of iron and bronze that Will kept looped around his belt. Maggie, whatever she was, seemed to be a servant of the Dark, source of all evil and the main antagonistic force of the story. Will was paralyzed and the Signs were almost stolen, but thankfully Will's mentor, Merriman, was there to banish the Witch and save Will. This instance of the story surprised me because it showed that the Dark has a much larger influence than Will first realized, stretching to even so-called "friends" of the family, and he would have to be extremely careful with who, or what he put his trust into.

Another surprise that startled me was when Will discovered the story behind the Walker, who to Will was simply the strange tramp who had been tasked with carrying one of the Signs. At one point in the story, Will and Merriman travel back in time to the year 1875 to a mansion in which people were celebrating, and the owner of the mansion, Miss Greythorne, assisted Will in obtaining the Sign of Wood. Other than retrieving the Sign of Wood, Will also found himself tasked with reading the BOOK OF GRAMARYE which contained a vast array of knowledge that was essential to Will in his training as an Old One, who are the servants of Light and primary protagonist force. Before reading the Book, Will meet Hawkin, who is apparently affiliated with Merriman in some way. It is discovered that Hawkin is a servant who Merriman who has brought out of his own time in order to unlock the spell of the Book. However, Maggie, the Dark Witch, was at the celebration. She tricked Hawkin into believing that Merriman and the Light were simply using him as a tool, nothing more. Hawkin, attracted to the thought of the Dark, made the choice of joining it as their liege man, and sealing his own doom. Later in the story, it is revealed that the Light had punished Hawkin, but not how. Finally, Will discovers that the Tramp, this strange, old feeble man who seemed so insignificant, was Hawkin. Serving

Pembroke Publishers © 2012 *Ban the Book Report* by Graham Foster ISBN 978-1-55138-264-7

Exemplar continued

his punishment for the Light, he was tasked with holding the Sign of Bronze and to walk the Earth endlessly with its burden until the next and last Old One, Will, came to retrieve it. This is the part of the novel that seriously shook me. I had no idea that the Walker, this character who seemed to be no more than a strange homeless old man, would have such a large impact on the story.

In conclusion, the surprises that THE DARK IS RISING threw my way were more than enough to keep me engaged to the story, not to mention the excellent style the story was written in. It is, overall, a brilliant novel, and I thoroughly enjoyed reading it. I hope to be able to pick up the next book in this series and continue the wicked story this book started.

Pembroke Publishers © 2012 *Ban the Book Report* by Graham Foster ISBN 978-1-55138-264-7

Talk-Show Interview

Watch a talk-show interview to note how interviewers ask probing questions that invite the subject to explain reasons for choices and beliefs.

1. What four or five key questions do you wish to pose to the author of your book?
2. How do you think that your author would respond to each of these questions?
3. Why do you think that these questions and answers are effective?

Name: _____   Date: _____

	I'm not there yet	I'm getting there	I'm there now
Information about the Book	My questions should be more clearly worded and my answers do not reveal reasons for the author's choices.	I present clearly worded questions and answers that offer adequate responses about the author's choices.	I present probing questions and insightful answers about the author's choices.
Reasoning	I am unable to explain why my questions and answers are effective.	I present adequate reasons about why my questions and answers are effective.	I present detailed reasons about why my questions and answers are effective.
Presentation	My questions and answers are not clearly worded. I am careless with spelling and grammar/usage.	My questions and answers are clearly worded. A few mistakes with spelling and grammar/usage distract my reader.	My questions and answers are effectively worded. I have few or no mistakes in spelling and grammar/usage.

Reading Completed

Book Title: _____   Author: _____

❑ I have read the entire book.
❑ I have read at least half of the book.
❑ I have read less than half of the book.
❑ I have read little or none of the book.

What I like best about my interview: _____

_____

My reading goal for my next book: _____

_____

Pembroke Publishers © 2012 *Ban the Book Report* by Graham Foster ISBN 978-1-55138-264-7

Talk-Show Interview

Book Title: *Touching Spirit Bear*   Author: Ben Mikaelsen

1. What inspired you to write a book about how nature can change a person's life so drastically?
Well, I own a black grizzly bear that I've been caring for about 10 years and I cannot imagine a day without him. He's become almost a member of the family. He's helped me through the difficult times in life and even when humans cannot help, he's always there for me. I guess that was my inspiration on how an animal, a part of nature, can help change us physically or internally with benefits along the way.

2. Why did you portray Cole the way you did?
Well, I first wanted to show how nature can change our characters or personalities so in the first half of the book I portrayed Cole as a cold hearted character who felt no remorse. Then his encounter with the spirit bear in a natural setting allowed him to change to become a caring, gentle person. The spirit bear concept is central to Cole's character development.

3. If you could change one thing in the novel, what would it be?
In the novel, I have a character named Peter join Cole on the island. I had mixed feelings about this part of the plot because Peter is only a minor character in the first part of the story. In addition, some readers might think that having Peter join Cole on the island is unrealistic and that no form of justice would allow that. However, I wanted to place Peter on the island to emphasize Cole's character development—his ability to apologize and to learn about true friendship.

4. Do you believe Circle Justice should be used in the real world?
Much as how Circle Justice is portrayed in the novel as a form of healing rather than punishment, I strongly support restorative justice systems. Therefore, I believe some people deserve second chances because they might not have known better. At some point in their lives they will need to re-enter society and Circle Justice in my opinion is the best way. I believe Circle Justice should be more recognized by the government and be used as an actual sentence to help treat offenders who are willing to change by isolating themselves for a year.

I chose these questions because I personally wanted them to be answered. The questions and answers were also based on my predictions and opinions since I believe that was what Ben Mikaelsen would have answered after reading his biography and his opinions about Circle Justice on the back of the book. If I were to be interviewing Ben Mikaelsen, I would pick these four questions since I believe these questions would get the best response.

Pembroke Publishers © 2012 *Ban the Book Report* by Graham Foster ISBN 978-1-55138-264-7

Exemplar continued

For the first question, I wanted to know what inspired him to write a book centring on changing a troubled person through nature.

For the second question, I wanted to know why did Ben Mikaelsen portrayed Cole the way he did and dramatically make him almost an entirely different person in the second half of the book.

For the third question, I wanted to know what part of the book Ben Mikaelsen would have changed. I believe he would have wanted to change the part where Peter joined Cole on the island since I believe it is unrealistic and no justice system would ever allow that.

For the last question, I wanted Ben Mikaelsen's own opinion on Circle Justice and if he wanted it to be used in real life. Since he did some research on Native American culture, I believe he must have had some opinion on whether Circle Justice should be an actual sentence used for offenders with the potential to change.

Pembroke Publishers © 2012 *Ban the Book Report* by Graham Foster ISBN 978-1-55138-264-7

Talk-Show Interview

Book Title: *In Spite of Killer Bees*   Author: Julie Johnson

1. In the book Agatha is portrayed as a troubled girl who thinks that her entire life is a movie. Why did you choose to make her character like that?
When I was creating the plot I realized the many hardships that Agatha was going through. I thought it would make sense to have Aggie pretend she was in a movie to escape the hardships of her life. In the book Agatha's sisters are always telling her to wake up and come to the real world. I think it seemed appropriate to have Aggie pretend to be in a movie since her entire life was in chaos. This was also based on what I do in my life; sometimes I escape reality and live inside whatever story I'm writing.

2. What does the title IN SPITE OF KILLER BEES mean to you?
To me, IN SPITE OF KILLER BEES means that even though life sometimes gives you hardships you just need to ignore it. It doesn't matter if life throws challenges like killer bees in your way. It means not giving up and not giving in. When I created the title I was thinking about all the difficulties that the main character, Agatha, went through. In the end she was still able to pull through and achieve a happy ending.

3. The book ends with Agatha directing the story like a movie. If you could change this ending, would you?
I wouldn't change the ending of the book because I think that the ending really relates to the book as a whole. All the problems have been solved and Aggie's family is happy again. Her life finally has a happy ending and Agatha's "movie" comes to reality. She's not directing movies in her head anymore—she's directing her real life.

4. When you were first writing the story did you intend for the mom to come back to the three girls?
No, I did not. I didn't think of the idea until the middle of writing the book. At first, I didn't want their mom to come back to them. In the book Agatha sort of expected her mom to come home and become the amazing mother that she always imagined since she was living in her "movie" world. I wanted Aggie to come to reality when she realized that their mom was never returning. But I also wanted the mom to come home just for the money that the three girls inherited. This would create a good plot with the mom disappointing the girls. Eventually I chose this idea but I tweaked it a little so that the mom turns out to be an appealing character in the end.

Pembroke Publishers © 2012 *Ban the Book Report* by Graham Foster ISBN 978-1-55138-264-7

Exemplar continued

I chose these questions because I was thinking a lot about them while I was reading the book and I actually wanted Julie Johnston to answer them. I did a little researching about Julie Johnston so that I could answer them as correctly as possible. I believe that the questions would really get her thinking and would receive a good response. Since I didn't know exactly how Julie would reply to my questions I predicted what she said from reading some of her other interview answers. I also based some of the answers on what I thought. If I were actually interviewing Julie Johnston I would choose these questions because I find them very thought provoking.

For the first question, I wanted to know why Agatha acted the way she did. The book never really explained why Aggie liked to pretend she was in a movie.

For the second question, I decided to ask about the title of the book because when I was first reading the book I didn't understand the title. I had to think about the title for a long time before I finally understood what it meant. Even then, I wasn't sure if my meaning was the same as what Julie Johnston intended it to be.

For the third question, I asked about the end of the book. I didn't really like how the book ended so I wanted the author's thoughts on the subject.

For the last question, I wanted to know if the author had any changing ideas as she was writing the story. I asked specifically about the mom because she was a character that interested me in the book.

Pembroke Publishers © 2012 *Ban the Book Report* by Graham Foster ISBN 978-1-55138-264-7

4 Written Response Assignments

Chapter 8 includes two additional written response options: Create a Social Media Page (page 96) and Write a Poem (page 97).

This section includes five assignments that encourage students to respond to reading in familiar written text forms: newspaper article, diary entry, revised ending or sequel chapter, letter, and eulogy.

Newspaper Headline and Article invites students to learn about the structure of newspaper articles. Teachers report that once students have learned about newspaper articles, they enjoy completing this assignment.

Diary Entry for a Character is another popular option for students. Many students find first-person commentary to be more comfortable than third-person options. In addition, many students enjoy pretending to be the character and writing in the character's role.

Revised Ending or Sequel Chapter is truly a challenging reading-response assignment. However, capable and imaginative students, usually voracious readers, often complete impressive work in rewriting the book's ending or writing a sequel chapter set six months to a year following the novel's final chapter. Students report that the sequel chapter assignment is easier when they write in the first-person.

Letter to the Author is another student favorite. Students seem willing to risk honest expression of their thoughts and emotions with the letter format.

Eulogy for a Major Character demands some teaching about eulogies, a format unfamiliar to many students. Students who work with exemplars similar to the two presented are more likely to attempt to write a eulogy.

Newspaper Headline and Article

After examining headlines and news stories, write a headline and news article for a major event in your novel. Be sure that your article answers H-W5 questions: *Who? What? Where? When? Why?* and *How?* Remember that the purpose of your headline is to draw attention to the news article in a brief and effective way. Sometimes headlines grab the reader's attention with the use of puns, humor, or alliteration. As you present your newspaper headline and article to others, be prepared to answer these questions:

1. Why is my headline effective?
2. How does my news story answer critical questions: *Who? What? Where? When? Why? How?*

Name: _____   Date: _____

	I'm not there yet	I'm getting there	I'm there now
Information about the Book	My newspaper article provides little information about the who, when, where, what, why, and how of the story. The headline is confusing.	My newspaper article contains most of the critical information about the who, where, when, what, why, and how of the story. My headline is informative.	My newspaper article presents all of the critical information about the who, where, when, what, why, and how of my story. My headline commands attention.
Reasoning	I am unable to explain why my article is complete and why my headline is effective.	I present a limited explanation about why my news article is complete and why my headline is effective.	I present a thorough explanation about why my news article is complete and why my headline is effective.
Presentation	My news article could more effectively organize the information.	My news article clearly organizes the information.	My news article effectively organizes the information.

Reading Completed

Book Title: _____   Author: _____

❏ I have read the entire book.
❏ I have read at least half of the book.
❏ I have read less than half of the book.
❏ I have read little or none of the book.

What I like best about my newspaper article: _____

_____

My goal for my next news article response or for my reading: _____

_____

Pembroke Publishers © 2012 *Ban the Book Report* by Graham Foster ISBN 978-1-55138-264-7

Newspaper Headline and Article

Book Title: *Touching Spirit Bear*   Author: Ben Mikaelsen

Young Offender Mauled by Bear on Remote Alaskan Island

Cole Matthews, a fifteen year old boy from Minneapolis was attacked by a bear last Thursday. The mauling occurred on a remote Alaskan island where the boy suffered broken ribs, a fractured pelvis, and a badly ripped and crushed arm.

Since the boy was alone on the island, help did not arrive until nearly a day after the attack when he was discovered in critical condition. He was brought back to the main island and treated by a native Tlingit nurse. From there, he was transported to a local hospital and treated for his wounds. "Cole is lucky to be alive, what happened to him would have killed most people," reported the Tlingit nurse who first treated the boy.

Local officials suggested that sympathy can be felt for this teen due to the circumstances for being on the island. He was not on the island by choice; instead, he was forcibly sent to the island to serve a one year banishment sentence for severely beating another boy from Minneapolis. Rather than being sentenced through the regular courts, this boy went through a justice system called "Circle Justice," which has been practiced by native tribes for many years. It is unknown if the boy will return to the island to finish his sentence. At the moment, Cole Matthews faces a slow medical recovery.

Newspaper Headline and Article

Book Title: *Harry Potter and the Prisoner of Azkaban*   Author: J.K. Rowling

Breakout From Azkaban

Cornelius Fudge, Minister Of Magic, reports that Sirius Black, mass murderer, has broken out from Azkaban Prison for Dark Wizards. He was convicted for the murder of one wizard, Peter Pettigrew, and a dozen muggles. He has been held in Azkaban for thirteen years and is accused of being he who must not be named's right hand follower.

Black escaped on July 3rd and his whereabouts are still unknown. If sighted he should not be approached as he is extremely dangerous. Instead, you should inform the ministry of magic immediately if you have any information as to where he is hiding. There will be a ten thousand galleon reward to the witch or wizard that provides us with information leading to the capture of this criminal.

It is still unknown how he has managed to escape Azkaban as he is the first person ever to do it. He is distinguishable by his shoulder length black hair, skinny face and maniacal expression of hate. Until he is found the Dementors of Azkaban will be stationed in all wizarding villages and schools including Hoggsmeade Village and the Hogwarts School of Witchcraft and Wizardry.

Sirius Black is considered dangerous and is to be avoided at all cost.

Diary Entry for a Character

Write a one-page diary entry for a character in your novel. Pretend to be the character and write in the first-person ("I"). Focus on identifying a conflict faced by the character and how the character felt about dealing with the conflict. Suggest how your character might have been changed by the experience.

1. Did you identify a conflict faced by your character?
2. Did you explain how your character dealt with the conflict?
3. Does your entry share details about how your character felt about dealing with the conflict?
4. Does your entry suggest how your character may have changed by the experience?

Name: _____   Date: _____

	I'm not there yet	I'm getting there	I'm there now
Information about the Book	My diary entry provides little information about my character's conflict and how my character deals with the conflict.	My diary entry adequately explains my character's conflict and how my character deals with the conflict.	My diary entry thoroughly explains my character's conflict and how my character deals with the conflict.
Reasoning	My diary entry presents little or no information about how my character felt and was changed by the conflict.	My diary entry presents adequate details about how my character felt and was changed by the conflicts.	My diary entry presents extensive details about how my character felt and was changed by the conflicts.
Presentation	My diary entry is not clearly worded. I am careless with spelling and grammar/usage.	My diary entry is clearly worded. A few mistakes with spelling and grammar/usage distract my reader.	My diary entry is effectively worded. I have few or no mistakes in spelling and grammar usage.

Reading Completed

Book Title: _____   Author: _____

❑ I have read the entire book.
❑ I have read at least half of the book.
❑ I have read less than half of the book.
❑ I have read little or none of the book.

What I like best about my diary entry: _____

_____

My reading goal for my next book: _____

_____

Pembroke Publishers © 2012 *Ban the Book Report* by Graham Foster ISBN 978-1-55138-264-7

Diary Entry for a Character

Book Title: *Harry Potter and the Order of the Phoenix*   Author: J.K. Rowling

When I heard that I got expelled from Hogwarts School, I was distraught. Luckily, I was trapped in my own room to face my punishment since my evil Uncle Vernon told me that I've already caused enough trouble for him and his annoying son, Dudley. It wasn't fair. I was only trying to protect Dudley from the Dementors but Uncle Vernon still blamed me for almost getting him killed. Next thing I know, I was visited by a group of wizards. They brought me to my godfather's house to discuss about the fact that Voldemort was back. I've known this for awhile now because I've been having nightmares and sometimes I feel really angry with the people I'm close to. When I was able to go back to Hogwarts, I learned that we had a new teacher named Delores Umbridge, who was replacing Severus Snape to teach us Defense against the Dark Arts. I find her very strict.

Weeks after, I was having many nightmares but this time, they were more disturbing. After Hermione and I blackmailed Professor Umbridge, the centaurs took her with them. The following day, my friends and I were after glass sphere that was named after me and Voldemort. Dementors arrived and we fought. I felt like this was the last time I would breathe and see my friends. Next thing I knew, my godfather arrived as well. While we were fighting the Dementors, somehow I got distracted by the sound of a glass shattering from the ground. When I looked up, I saw his my godfather's own cousin kill him with a curse. I cried to myself in pain while I tried to run after his cousin. I felt infuriated for the first time. This was my first time seeing a family member die in front of me. I can't stand the thought of seeing him in my mind all the time. It feels that I'm responsible for what happened back there and I will never ever forgive myself.

Pembroke Publishers © 2012 *Ban the Book Report* by Graham Foster ISBN 978-1-55138-264-7

Diary Entry for a Character

Book Title: *Eragon*   Author : Christopher Paolini

Note: I chose a part of my book where I thought Eragon experienced intense problems and emotions. He needed to make the decision of what he's going to do next after the battle.

Being reminded constantly of what just happened was the last thing I wanted. Violent, cruel images of the battle flashed through my head as my head was still trying to put things in place. My mind felt hopeless as more horrible and painful images popped into my brain. It was impossible to clear my mind. The memories seemed to just burst and dissolve, leaving me to look at my accomplishments and failures, realizing that I lost a lot of people whom I loved. Yet I was given Saphira and many other great gifts. And for once I felt proud of who I was and my self-confidence grew. I was still too weak to clear my mind completely, but all I could think of was where would I go now? Who would show me the way? Without Brom, there was no one to guide or teach me.

I heard a voice that was calling out to me. He told me that he was Osthato Chetowa, the mourning sage. I realized that he was the one blocking the pain. He talked to me about meeting him before it was too late, that he had the answer to all my questions, and that Arya would lead me to him in Ellesmera, land of elves. His voice disappeared. Still feeling lightheaded, I was awakened by Angela. I almost forgot about Saphira. As Murtagh and Arya entered the room, I was happy to see them but I drowned them with questions since I had been sleeping for about a day and a half, and I didn't know what was going on. As they answered my questions I remembered something from when I was unconscious. The man had said, "Think of what you have done and rejoice, for you have rid the land of a great evil. You have wrought a deed no one else could. Many are in your debt…" A measure of peace and satisfaction consoled me.

People have started to call me Eragon the Shade Slayer after I defeated Durza, and now I know that these people count on me to help them. Once I destroyed Galbatorix, these people don't have to be afraid anymore and they can live their own independent lives without worrying. I know that I can't help everyone and that I have to sacrifice some things, and I realize now that I have to be more responsible and accept my duties because I am a rider. I had become what Ajihad wanted: an authority independent of any king or leader. I have decided to go and listen to the Mourning Sage's words; I will go to him and learn.

Pembroke Publishers © 2012 *Ban the Book Report* by Graham Foster ISBN 978-1-55138-264-7

Revised Ending or Sequel Chapter

Rewrite the ending of your novel or write a sequel chapter set months or years after your novel's final chapter. Focus on what has changed or what is different for at least one character as a result of the character's dealing with the novel's central conflict. Attach a paragraph to explain why you made the changes in the ending or why you included the details and events in your sequel chapter.

Name: _____   Date: _____

	I'm not there yet	I'm getting there	I'm there now
Information about the Book	My revised ending or sequel chapter provides little or no indication of what has changed or is different for at least one character.	My revised ending or sequel chapter provides some indication of what has changed or is different for at least one character.	My revised ending or sequel chapter clearly illustrates what has changed or is different for at least one character.
Reasoning	I need to add reasons to explain my revised chapter or sequel chapter.	I present adequate reasoning for my revised ending or sequel chapter.	I present detailed reasoning for my revised ending or sequel chapter.
Presentation	My response is not clearly worded. I am careless with spelling and grammar/usage.	My response is clearly worded. A few mistakes with spelling and grammar/usage distract my reader.	My response is effectively worded. I have few or no mistakes in spelling and grammar/usage.

Reading Completed

Book Title: _____   Author: _____

❑ I have read the entire book.
❑ I have read at least half of the book.
❑ I have read less than half of the book.
❑ I have read little or none of the book.

What I like best about my revised ending or sequel chapter: _____

_____

My reading goal for my next book: _____

_____

Pembroke Publishers © 2012 *Ban the Book Report* by Graham Foster ISBN 978-1-55138-264-7

Revised Ending

Book Title: *Specials*   Author: Scott Westerfeld

Tally could feel the hovercrafts coming even before she saw them. It would only be a matter of minutes before the fire would start. "But cities don't have wars!" screamed Tally.

"We started something huge, Tally," said Shay. "Ever since that day that we met up with David, something had been waiting to explode for the longest time. People had been longing for this to happen and all they needed was our push to wake them up. But it is like waking up a sleeping beast. At first it might seem silent and calm but it will only be a matter of time before it will pounce."

Tally stood there in silence, listening to Shay and looking out at Diego. "And our time is up. Now we have to finish what we started. We have to end this war but this time end it right."

"Come," whispered Shay holding out her hand to Tally. Tally hesitated, not sure what she should do. "Come on, Tally, please," pleaded Shay. "If not for me then do it for Zane. You know this is what he would want."

Tally didn't move. She was thinking about Zane. How he used to be and how he was now. How he was before. All she wanted was to be with him and he surely still hated her after what she had done. Suddenly the fire started and an icy-making scream shot up from Diego. "Agh, come on, Tally, wha—," shrieked Shay. "What are you waiting for!"

Another small hovercraft was coming up low just ahead. "That," said Tally. She turned on her skintenna and jumped onto her hoverboard. Tally could hear Shay breathing through the skintenna as they inched towards the hovercraft. "On my cue," whispered Tally, "jump." Tally waited until it was almost too late before silently whispering, "Now." They both jumped in unison onto the hovercraft just in time. If they had jumped a second before or after they would have missed their landing.

The hovercraft sped along not seeming to even notice the small bump as Tally and Shay jumped on. Tally's mind felt icy and clear. The few seconds of freefall just before contact with the craft was enough to make her mind icy. The hovercraft had reached Diego and had started to open fire. Tally braced herself to break in and stop the craft but Shay could tell what she was planning to do.

"Wait," cried Shay, "Go for the head hovercraft. I want this thing ended fast and not with us in the flames."

Tally nodded and waited until the craft was closer to another to jump. It took three more jumps before landing on top of the main hovercraft. Shay landed a second after Tally. Tally dug her nails deep into the glass and metal coverings and it started shredding quickly. Every second wasted was another second for the Specials to realize that they were on top of them. Tally could see Dr. Cable inside which only made her claw harder. As soon as she made a hole, Tally started kicking, sending chunks of glass into the hovercraft. If they hadn't noticed them on top yet, then

Pembroke Publishers © 2012 *Ban the Book Report* by Graham Foster ISBN 978-1-55138-264-7

Exemplar continued

they certainly did now. Specials started swarming around trying to get at them but Dr. Cable raised her hand. "Stop," she said, "Let them come in!"

Tally and Shay dropped inside slowly and froze. Tally's mind was suddenly non-icy. What exactly had she walked herself into?

"This is between you and me now, Dr. Cable," snapped Tally. "I don't believe that we need to kill anyone else today."

Dr. Cable smiled sickly, "But of course," she said. Dr. Cable tossed Tally a knife. "Go ahead, Tally, start the fight. Finish me off. It won't make any difference in the end."

The knife seemed to be coming to Tally just waiting for her to pick it up. "Oh, but you see, Dr. Cable, it will," said Tally. She ran at her not bothering to get the knife and lashed out at Dr. Cable's throat. Dr. Cable crumpled down in front of Tally, still alive, but barely.

"One day you will regret this, Tally. One day you will regret this all," she snapped and with her final words, died.

Quickly the other Specials were on Shay and were coming towards Tally. She grabbed under the dashboard and ripped out as many wires as she could. One lucky grab had been the one and the hovercraft quickly started to fall. All the other crafts stopped firing as the craft started crashing into the ground. It burst into flames. Tally felt burning ripping and pain like she had never felt before. And then she went blank.

Tally woke up but refused to open her eyes. First she ran her fingernails across her fingers. Still sharp. Then she ran her tongue across her teeth. Still points. Tally opened her eyes to green lush everywhere. She heard a twig snap behind her and quickly she jumped up and turned. Suddenly Tally felt icier that she had ever felt. She couldn't tell whether or not she was angry, happy, over-joyed, pained or thrilled. She couldn't even tell how she had gotten where she was or even if she was still alive. All she could tell was that she was icy. That and she was with David.

I changed the ending to what I did because I wanted there to be more of a fight. When I was reading the book, I thought there would be a bit more excitement and mystery. Also, I wanted Tally to end up with David, but I didn't want Zane dead. I wanted there to be unanswered questions to let the reader guess what could happen for themselves. Such as what happened to Zane and Diego? Was Tally alive? And what had happened after the crash? As well, I didn't want Tally to end up with David because she had no choice. I wanted her to be with him because she still felt something inside.

Pembroke Publishers © 2012 *Ban the Book Report* by Graham Foster ISBN 978-1-55138-264-7

Sequel Chapter

Book Title: *Lockdown: Escape from Furnace*   Author: Alexander Gordon Smith

A year has passed since I saw Carl Donovan. I remember seeing his face when the men in black suits dragged him from our cell. I remember the time when I promised him that I would come back. That I would come back to the hell-hole known as Furnace Penitentiary. But I could never forget the time when I saw hope for us, the day when I discovered the exit. I was thrilled. Knowing that there was a way out was the best thing that ever happened to me. We went through and we ran until our legs were bleeding. We were dodging debris, claws, and bullets all the time while Satan's minions were chasing us. We didn't think about anything else. We just ran and ran until we gained distance from them.

After all this time, we were still cowering from the very sight of Furnace. But when I gasped that first fresh air, I knew we were in the right direction. We went out and I saw the trees and the stars, all swaying and shining in a way that I couldn't understand. There was a peaceful silence in the air. I let my feet touch the grass and it was good. A breath of fresh air refreshed my aching body. Finally, we were out. Finally the guards knew that there was an escape in the penitentiary. Freedom was a choice none of us would agree on, but we did it.

Unfortunately, we were not out of the woods yet. The guards were still hot on our trail and were trying everything in their power to haul us back and turn us into monsters. My spine chilled from the very thought of it. But I knew that once upon a time, I promised a boy freedom and I was never going to give up until I fulfilled that promise.

I made the changes because at last there was hope for this boy to save him and everyone else who was innocent and locked inside Furnace Penitentiary. Alex now had a chance to clear his name from what he did not do—murder his friend.

Reasons for my choices:

After his time in jail, I noticed that Alex hadn't felt anything good in his time in Furnace. I changed that because now there is a ray of hope shining on Alex to get out of this nightmare.

Letter to the Author

Write a letter to the author of your book, even if your author is not alive or is at an unknown address. Present comments, questions, and requests for the author, as well as reasons for your comments, questions, and/or requests.

Name: _____   Date: _____

	I'm not there yet	I'm getting there	I'm there now
Information about the Book	My letter presents few or no comments, questions, and/or requests.	My letter includes comments, questions, and /or requests.	My letter presents detailed comments, questions, and/or requests.
Reasoning	My letter provides no reasons for my comments, questions, and/or requests.	My letter provides limited reasons for my comments, questions, and/or requests.	My letter provides thoughtful reasons for my comments, questions, and/or requests.
Presentation	My letter is disorganized and not clearly worded. I am careless with spelling and grammar/usage.	My letter is organized and clearly worded. A few mistakes with spelling and grammar/usage distract my reader.	My letter is well-organized and effectively worded with few or no mistakes in spelling or grammar/usage.

Reading Completed

Book Title: _____   Author: _____

❑ I have read the entire book.
❑ I have read at least half of the book.
❑ I have read less than half of the book.
❑ I have read little or none of the book.

What I like best about my letter to the author: _____

_____

My reading goal for my next book: _____

_____

Pembroke Publishers © 2012 *Ban the Book Report* by Graham Foster ISBN 978-1-55138-264-7

Letter to the Author

Book Title: *Invisible City*   **Author:** M.G. Harris

Dear M. G. Harris:

I have recently read INVISIBLE CITY, the first of your series The Joshua Files. The novel took me deeper into a subject fairly unknown to me—the Mayan civilization. Yes, your book is fictional; yet it developed a sense of curiosity about factual information within me. I found myself wanting to uncover more about this lost society. Please allow me to share my observations.

Your storyline started out slowly but quickly rose in interest when Josh had met Ollie. Then everything was set into place, especially when the couple arrived in Mexico and met Camila, Josh's older secret half-sister. When I read about Camila's death, I was so shocked! The car chase leading up to it kept me on the edge. Everything after that was an amazing, accelerating adventure—from Josh almost dying in the jungle to the end, where he finds out that the runaway in the jungle is his arranged wife to be. You are so capable of sustaining interest in your readers!

Even though I'm a girl, I feel as though I can feel what Josh felt because of how you chose your words. All the anger and determination that derived from his father's death to the sweet relief of having the codex in his possession captured me.

Now I am curious about how you were inspired to write a piece about the possible apocalypse. Have you even been to the Mayan ruins? If so, are they very close to what you described in your book? Do the events relate to your personal life in any way?

I was totally hooked when Josh fulfilled his duty of finding the Ix codex. For him to finally end the hunt for this codex, which had been killing generations of his family, was a totally satisfying ending. Of course you have led me to the beginning of a new book, the second of your series!

Thank you for writing such a thrilling adventure. I hope to read your next book soon.

Sincerely,
Amy Tang

Pembroke Publishers © 2012 *Ban the Book Report* by Graham Foster ISBN 978-1-55138-264-7

Letter to the Author

Book Title: *The Perks of Being a Wallflower*   Author: Stephan Chbosky

Dear Stephan Chbosky:

I am writing to share my views about your novel THE PERKS OF BEING A WALLFLOWER. THE PERKS OF BEING A WALLFLOWER is my favorite book of all time! I discovered it last year through a friend and since then have never felt the same about a book. Within each page, each line, a new emotion rose from my core. This book had my insides churning, had me constantly wiping away tears from my eyes and of course, in places had me smiling smiles and laughing. I did not once put the book down out of boredom. I was hooked until the very end. I wasn't in the greatest place mentally last year, but this book gave me hope, in friends, school and myself. It made me believe that there was a brighter future.

I liked the approach you chose; it made me feel more emotionally involved than a standard novel would. I felt like Charlie was actually writing to me, that he was an everyday person and not some fictional character out of a book. I suppose I'm fond of the book because it's reality: it's believable and I can relate to most of the emotions that Charlie felt. I found the build up for Charlie and Sam's relationship kind of slow but I guess if it went any faster, I would have got the impression that she was sleazy. Patrick's being gay was also an interesting touch. If it wasn't pointed out, I would have read the entire book with the impression that he was straight. My favorite quote just happens to be from your book too, "And in that moment, I swear we were infinite." And I have the poem on page 72 memorized word for word. Your novel is truly a work of art.

I hope that you continue to write books because you are an incredible author and if possible, I would like to suggest a sequel. It could be about Charlie's senior year. I would like to see how much has changed between the trio. I wish you the best in your career and thank you very much for taking the time to read the letter of your best fan!

Yours truly,
Petra Flynn

Pembroke Publishers © 2012 *Ban the Book Report* by Graham Foster ISBN 978-1-55138-264-7

Eulogy for a Major Character

From the point of view of a character in your novel, write a eulogy for a main character in the book. A eulogy is a tribute usually presented at funerals or memorial services, but it is not restricted to funerals. Read examples of eulogies online to become familiar with the form. As you present your eulogy to others, be prepared to point out the following:

1. Where you describe your relationship with the person.
2. Where you describe interests, key events, and/or achievements in the life of the subject.
3. Where you describe special qualities of the subject.
4. Where you describe how the person was important to you and others.

Name: _____   Date: _____

	I'm not there yet	I'm getting there	I'm there now
Information about the Book	My eulogy presents little information about the person and little information on how the deceased influenced me and others.	My eulogy presents limited important information about the person with attention to how the deceased influenced me and others.	My eulogy presents adequate important information about the person with an emphasis on how the deceased influenced me and others.
Reasoning	I present few reasons to explain why the person is important to me and others.	I present reasons to explain why the person is important to me and others.	I present extensive reasons to explain why the person is important to me and others.
Presentation	My eulogy is disorganized. I am careless with spelling and grammar/usage.	My eulogy is organized. A few mistakes in spelling and grammar/usage distract my reader.	My eulogy is effectively organized. I have few or no mistakes in spelling and grammar/usage.

Reading Completed

Book Title: _____   Author: _____

❑ I have read the entire book.
❑ I have read at least half of the book.
❑ I have read less than half of the book.
❑ I have read little or none of the book.

What I like best about my eulogy: _____

_____

My reading goal for my next book: _____

_____

Pembroke Publishers © 2012 *Ban the Book Report* by Graham Foster ISBN 978-1-55138-264-7

Eulogy for a Major Character

Book Title: *Leonardo's Shadow*   Author: Christopher Grey

Giacomo of Pisa passed away in the spring of 1543, at the age of 61. He died of natural causes. He was born in 1482 in Milan, Italy. Giacomo was the servant of Leonardo da Vinci for eight years before becoming his apprentice in 1597. Giacomo also studied mixing colors with Messer Tombi of Milan. He was chosen to fly da Vinci's famous "flying machine" at age 15, becoming the first man to ever fly.

In early 1400, Giacomo married Emelia Benedetti. Emelia and Giacomo had three children and were married 44 years. Their first child, Juggo, was born in 1500 in Milan; Giacomo and Emilia's second child, their only daughter, Margarita, was born in 1504 with their youngest, Pluto, in 1506. The last two children were born in Pisa.

As a child Giacomo did not know his real parents but was raised by Leonardo as his servant. He was saved by Leonardo after falling off the cathedral roof. He suffered another mishap when he was accused of being a thief. Giacomo would clean the house, run errands and take care of business accounts for Leonardo. Occasionally, he even helped on some of Leonardo's famous paintings, including the legendary Last Supper, in which his face was the model of the disciple John.

Giacomo moved from Milan to Pisa in 1502 after studying art with Leonardo for two years to open up his own art studio. Over the years, he became one of the most famous painters in all of Italy, because of his unique style that was a mixture of da Vinci's with his own twists. Some even compared him to his world renowned teacher, Leonardo.

Giacomo could always be found at his desk sketching and welcomed all of his many visitors with a firm handshake and a warm smile. Giacomo was known as an honest, hardworking man.

Giacomo is survived by his loving wife Emilia, his three beloved children, Juggo, Margarita and Pluto. He will be missed by his recent grandchildren, Filipa and Giovanni. He was pre-deceased by Caterina, his fellow servant who showed him the ropes as a child and who is buried at the San Georgio church. He also leaves Leonardo da Vinci, Giacomo's longtime master and teacher, and Giacomo's childhood friends, Renzo and Claudio.

We will all greatly miss his sense of humor and his never-ending passion for the arts. We will be having a celebration of Giacomo's great life at Santa Maria delle Grazie where he will be buried next to his all time favorite painting, The Last Supper.

Pembroke Publishers © 2012 *Ban the Book Report* by Graham Foster ISBN 978-1-55138-264-7

Eulogy for a Major Character

Book Title: *Bang*   Author: Norah McClintock

Mr. Richard Braithwaite was a saint. He was known to everybody as Rich. Rich he was with soul, humor, and passion for his community.

Richard would come and spend his Sundays playing the keys for me and the rest of the nursing home. He would play everybody's favorites, from Mozart to Bon Jovi. He reminded me of my son—tall, strongly built, very creative and clever with words; he was quite the intellect too.

He came to the United States from Trinidad with nothing more than a dime in his pocket and a drive to succeed. Richard worked many jobs on top of his volunteering. He worked in the construction field. However, he was best known for his cooking of Caribbean food. Richard had many talents. When the elementary school held a breakfast club, he worked his magic in the kitchen.

Such a kind man! Mr. Braithwaite had a knack with animals. He volunteered at the humane society as a dog walker. I would see him walk by occasionally with four or so dogs pulling him onward. Richard did so much for the community and I was happily surprised to hear he also coached a local soccer team! It's so wonderful to see young adults get involved in our neighborhood.

Mr. Braithwaite worked diligently to buy the canteen van that he was recently driving. The children on the beach simply loved his ice cream cones and cold pop.

This young gentleman, Rich, had a very strong heart. He had absolutely no tolerance for violence or bullying. It feels like yesterday that he was telling me about how he saw some young children on the swings getting harassed by some teenagers and boy did he tell those teenagers off!

Since Rich had very few rights when he first made his voyage to our town, he shared a strong belief for equality and fairness for the people of our neighborhood. He filled the streets with joy and spread his knowledge like a wildfire. Our town will be forever grateful for what he has contributed and shared with us. No matter where he is, he will never leave our hearts. We will be reunited someday. The celebration of his life will be held at the church where he came for direction; just as we came to him.

Pembroke Publishers © 2012 *Ban the Book Report* by Graham Foster ISBN 978-1-55138-264-7

5 Illustration and Graphic Representation Assignments

Chapter 8 includes two additional opportunities to illustrate or represent a book: Scrapbook or Backpack Collection (page 100) and Award Certificate for the Author (page 98).

This section presents four assignments focused on illustration or representation as a reading-response option. Each assignment challenges students to explain their choices in the illustration or graphic representation. Words and images must work together to suggest meaning.

Alternate Cover for My Book works best when students engage in discussion about illustrators' choices on book covers. If students identify and discuss examples of effective book covers, they learn to make deliberate choices in their own illustrations. The challenge for students to explain their choices in a written statement attached to the cover is an important part of the assignment, in that it reveals the thoughtfulness of the choices.

Five-Point Recap appeals to many students. Students enjoy the challenge of choosing one word to capture the focus of the novel, two words to describe the conflict, and other challenges that limit the number of words in the response. In addition, the assignment works well for students who enjoy artistic expression.

Map or Timeline for My Book presents two options to students. Each option works well with certain books and not for others. The map assignment works best for books in which the setting is critically important and in which the author presents many details about the setting; for example, fantasy books that present details of worlds very different from our own. The timeline works best for books that present a sequence of events related to dates or historical events; for example, biographies and historical fiction (the exemplar for the assignment organizes important events in the life of Odysseus in the timeline categories Before the Trojan War, During the Trojan War, and After the Trojan War).

Picturing Textual Details is popular with a variety of students. It is the most straightforward of the assignments presented in this section. Students illustrate two or three key events in the book. Note that students may draw, collect, or print the illustrations. Therefore, the assignment can be attempted by students who do not consider themselves to be artistically talented.

Alternate Cover for My Book

After examining the covers of several books and noting effective features of book covers, prepare an alternate cover for your book. With your teacher, decide whether you will include a back cover as well as a front cover. Attach a written explanation for your choices of images, words, and print size and shape.

1. What important information am I emphasizing?
2. How do I make the book cover interesting?

Name: _____   Date: _____

	I'm not there yet	I'm getting there	I'm there now
Information about the Book	My cover illustrations and information provide little information about important features in the book.	My cover illustrations and information provide limited guidance about the subject, conflict, or important features of the book.	My cover illustrations and information emphasize the subject, conflict, or important features of the book.
Reasoning	I am unable to explain why I included illustrations and information, and how I made the cover interesting.	I present an adequate explanation about why I included illustrations and information, and how I made the cover interesting.	I present a thorough explanation about why I included illustrations and information, and how I made the cover interesting.
Presentation	The illustrations and words on the cover are not placed to emphasize key points.	I have organized the illustrations and words to organize key points.	I have organized the illustration and words to emphasize key points clearly and effectively.

Reading Completed

Book Title: _____   Author: _____

❑ I have read the entire book.
❑ I have read at least half of the book.
❑ I have read less than half of the book.
❑ I have read little or none of the book.

What I like best about my book cover: _____

_____

My reading goal for my next book cover or my reading: _____

_____

Pembroke Publishers © 2012 *Ban the Book Report* by Graham Foster ISBN 978-1-55138-264-7

Alternate Cover for My Book

Book Title: *Touching Spirit Bear*   Author: Ben Mikaelsen

My cover of TOUCHING SPIRIT BEAR includes the scene where Cole physically touches the spirit bear. This scene is very significant to the whole novel because it basically represents the title TOUCHING SPIRIT BEAR. This scene is where Cole had been previously mauled by the spirit bear and as he lies down being semi-immobile, the Spirit Bear comes back again. Cole, wanting to feel what the animal that would have ended his life felt like, touches the Spirit Bear. Around the title, I drew several symbols that were introduced in the novel. There is a circle which represents the connection between humans and nature, a stick which represents the different ends of happiness and anger, and a flame which represents anger being built up. These symbols emphasize meaningful ideas in the novel. I didn't color the original cover, because the bark-like background already makes the cover look attractive. The pattern makes the whole book cover seem mysterious and forest-like which matches the theme of a secluded island. I also tried to make the cover as realistic as possible and used some shading in order to make the cover more eye-catching. The shading also makes up for the fact that I didn't color the cover.

Pembroke Publishers © 2012 *Ban the Book Report* by Graham Foster ISBN 978-1-55138-264-7

Alternate Cover for My Book

Book Title: *Old Turtle and the Broken Truth*   Author: Douglas Wood

I am making an alternate book cover for the story OLD TURTLE AND BROKEN TRUTH. I want to make an alternate book cover because to me the original book cover was a little plain.

I'm trying to emphasize the word "truth" and the little girl more. The little girl is important because she is the protagonist. To me the word "truth" wasn't emphasized enough in the original book cover and that is why I made the image larger and added another picture of it.

The book has a lot to say about the meaning of truth and of broken truths. The cover should point to these topics.

To make your book cover interesting, you can put an illustration of the problem of the plot. My illustration of the heart does this. The cover builds up suspense by making the reader wonder about the crack in the heart.

Five-Point Recap

Complete your five-point recap, filling in the boxes in the template.

1. Choose one word that captures the focus of the novel.
2. Use no more than two words to describe the major conflict of the novel.
3. Identify the three most interesting characters in the novel.
4. Use up to four words to suggest another title for the novel.
5. Illustrate or explain your favorite part of the text.

6. Why did you make these choices? Write brief explanations for each of your choices in the five-point recap.

Rubric

Name: _____   Date: _____

	I'm not there yet	I'm getting there	I'm there now
Information about the Book	My five-point recap does not follow the format requirement of the assignment.	My five-point recap follows the format requirements most of most of the five points.	My five-point recap completely follows the format requirements for each of the five points.
Reasoning	I need to add reasons to explain my choices of words and illustrations.	I include adequate reasoning. I need to add detail to explain my choices of words and illustration	I present detailed reasoning for my choices of words and illustration.
Presentation	My response is disorganized and not clearly worded. I am careless with spelling and grammar/usage.	My response is organized and clearly worded. A few mistakes with spelling and grammar/usage distract my reader.	My response is well-organized and effectively worded with few or no mistakes in spelling or grammar/usage.

Reading Completed

Book Title: _____   Author: _____

❑ I have read the entire book.
❑ I have read at least half of the book.
❑ I have read less than half of the book.
❑ I have read little or none of the book.

What I like best about my response: _____

_____

My reading goal for my next book: _____

_____

Five-Point Recap

Book Title: *Underground to Canada*   **Author:** Barbara Smucker

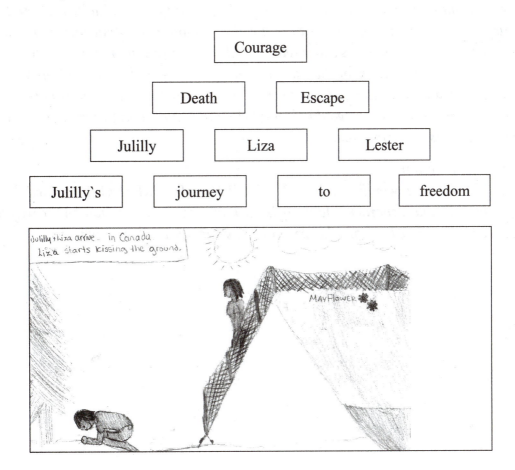

Courage
The word I think describes the book is courage. Why? Courage is what Julilly, Liza, Adam and Lester have to escape slavery. If anybody had caught them, they would have been whipped so many times they would be covered in scars, maybe even die from it. The two girls and two boys needed courage to travel in Mississippi at Massa Riley's plantation and end up in St. Catharines, Canada. They had to deal with new experiences they had never seen or done before. It was risky and used up all the courage they had.

Death and Escape
The two major conflicts of this novel are Adam's death and escaping slavery in Mississippi. I chose these because Adam's death is more than just a friend dying. He was like a real family member of Julilly. Julilly was very sad: her heart probably sank to the bottom of her body. Escaping slavery at the Riley's Plantation was the main goal. During the escape, Julilly did not know what dangers would happen to her and her friends.

Pembroke Publishers © 2012 *Ban the Book Report* by Graham Foster ISBN 978-1-55138-264-7

Exemplar continued

Julilly and Liza and Lester
I think the three most interesting characters are Julilly, Liza and Lester. Julilly is interesting because she is the one who is less serious than the others, more risk-taking and with more courage. Julilly is also interesting as she is selfless and kind, so you are more likely to want to be like her. I picked Liza and Lester for the same reasons (not because both of their names have the same letter!). They are sometimes quiet but some how I wanted to know more about them. Liza and Lester were loyal friends that would always help Julilly and stood by her side. I would want these three characters to be my friends.

Julilly's Journey to Freedom
Another title for the novel would be JULILLY'S JOURNEY TO FREEDOM. I picked this title because Julilly is the main character. Journey is the huge adventure she had on the way to Canada. Freedom is a free life from slavery and Canada's free land everywhere.

Pembroke Publishers © 2012 *Ban the Book Report* by Graham Foster ISBN 978-1-55138-264-7

Five-Point Recap

Book Title: *Warrior Cats: Darkest Hour*   Author: Erin Hunter

Battle

| Betrayal | Death |

| Firestar | Tigerstar | Scourge |

| The | War | of | Bloodclan |

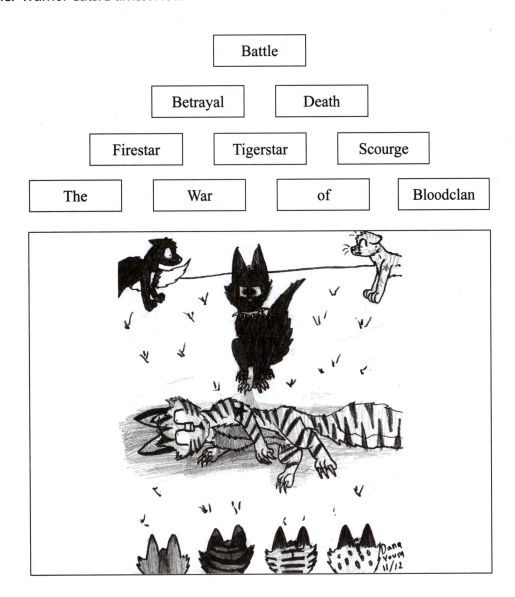

Battle
I chose this word because there is a lot of fighting in the book WARRIOR CATS: DARKEST HOUR. The word describes the book perfectly because at the end of the book, the four warrior clans Shadowclan, Thunderclan, Windclan, and Riverclan have to battle against a roughly organized group of stray cats called "Bloodclan" and their tyrannical leader Scourge.

Betrayal/Death
I chose the word "betrayal" because there is a lot of betrayal in this book. A cat named Darkstripe tried to murder a young kit (kitten) who was only still 4 moons (months) old.

Pembroke Publishers © 2012 *Ban the Book Report* by Graham Foster ISBN 978-1-55138-264-7

Exemplar continued

Scourge betrayed Tigerstar and killed him. After Tigerstar was dead, Scourge and Bloodclan tried to take over the forest.

I chose "death" because a lot of cats die in this book. Those cats include Tigerstar, Stonefur, Scourge, Firestar's first life (Clan leaders have nine lives), Whitestorm, Bone and many more.

Firestar/Tigerstar/Scourge

Firestar is the main character of the Warriors series. He is also the leader of Thunderclan. Firestar was taken into Thunderclan as a kitten and trained until he earned the rank of clan leader. Firestar is the one who killed Scourge and saved the forest. Firestar is a ginger tom with darker ginger stripes, a light belly and bright green eyes.

Tigerstar is the leader of Shadowclan and was exiled from Thunderclan because he was a traitor who killed many cats. Tigerstar brought Bloodclan into the forest because he wanted to use them for their evil doings and kill the leader Scourge, but soon Scourge killed him instead, taking all 9 lives with one claw blow. Tigerstar is a dark brown tom with black stripes, a white belly and amber eyes.

Scourge is the maniacal killer and leader of Bloodclan. He is a murderer who leads with power and fear rather than wisdom and courage. (Cool, right?) Scourge is a pure black tom cat with a purple collar ringed with the teeth of dogs and cats he has killed and dog teeth over his real claws. His right paw is white and he has piercing icy blue eyes.

The War of the Bloodclan

I chose this different title because there is a war for dominance over the forest with Bloodclan vs. the other clans together calling themselves "Lionclan."

Pembroke Publishers © 2012 *Ban the Book Report* by Graham Foster ISBN 978-1-55138-264-7

Map or Timeline for My Book

In some books, setting is a very important feature. For these books, you might choose to create a map to illustrate important locations for the action in the story.

1. Complete a web search to find examples of maps.
2. Create a map to illustrate important details of setting from your book.
3. Write one or two paragraphs to explain the importance of the details you have included in your map.

In many books, dates and the chronological order of events are important. For such books, you might choose to create a timeline to review the sequence of critical events.

1. Complete a web search to find examples of timelines.
2. Create a timeline (from left to right or top to bottom) to illustrate the sequence and dates of important events in your book.
3. Write one or two paragraphs to explain the importance of the details you have included in your timeline.

Name: _____   Date: _____

	I'm not there yet	I'm getting there	I'm there now
Information about the Book	My map or timeline presents few critical details about setting or key events.	My map or timeline presents most of the critical details about setting or key events.	My map or timeline presents all of the critical details about setting or key events.
Presentation	My map or timeline lacks neatness and visual appeal.	My map or timeline is neat but could be more visually appealing.	My map or timeline is neat and visually appealing.

Reading Completed

Book Title: _____   Author: _____

❑ I have read the entire book.
❑ I have read at least half of the book.
❑ I have read less than half of the book.
❑ I have read little or none of the book.

What I like best about my map or timeline: _____

_____

My reading goal for my next book: _____

_____

Pembroke Publishers © 2012 *Ban the Book Report* by Graham Foster ISBN 978-1-55138-264-7

Map for My Book

Book Title: *Ashes, Ashes*   Author: Jo Treggiari

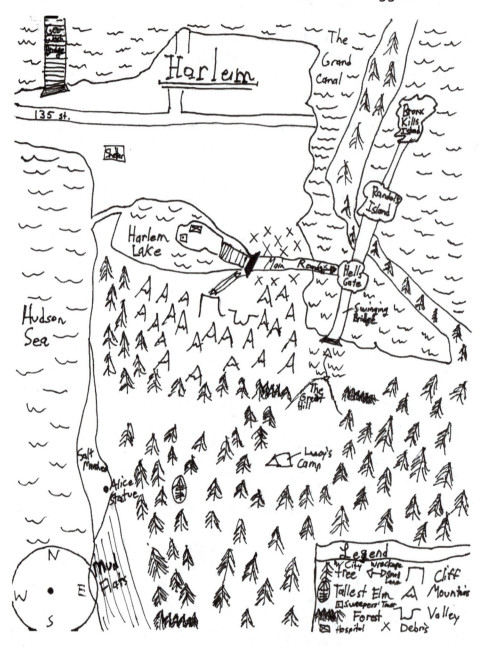

I made a map because I think that everyone imagines things differently. The author may think of the setting one way, I another and every single one of us will never imagine the setting the same way as someone else. So I decided to do my take on the author's description of the setting. I have illustrated important details in the story's setting.

Timeline for my Book

Book Title: *Tales from the Odyssey*   Author: Mary Pope Osborne

Critical Events in the Life of Odysseus

Before the Trojan War

> *Birth of his son.*
> *Odysseus leaves for Troy to save Helen (Greek Queen).*

During the Trojan War

> *Odysseus rescues Helen after 10 years of battle.*

After the War

> *Odysseus finds a giant named Polyphemus and blinds him to escape from his cave.*
> *Odysseus reveals his true identity to Polyphemus and puts a curse on him and all his men that they will never reach home alive.*
> *Odysseus and his men get into a huge wind storm due to this curse.*
> *A goddess named Circe tells Odysseus that the only way he'll ever get home is if he goes to the land of the dead and talks to the spirit of Tiresias, a fortune teller.*
> *Tiresias warns Odysseus and all his men of what they'll find on their journey home and tells them how to safely get home.*

Historians are uncertain about the exact dates of the Trojan War. The best I can do is to show important events in the life of Odysseus as they relate to the Trojan War—events before, during and after the war.

Pembroke Publishers © 2012 *Ban the Book Report* by Graham Foster ISBN 978-1-55138-264-7

Picturing Textual Details

Draw, collect or print two or three pictures to represent key episodes from your book. Label the image to indicate the episode. For each image, attach a paragraph to explain how the image illustrates a key feature of the book and how the image suggests an emotion related to the book.

Name: _____   Date: _____

	I'm not there yet	I'm getting there	I'm there now
Reasoning	I provide little or no explanation about how the images connect to the episode and how each image suggests an emotion.	I adequately explain how the images connect to the episodes and how each image suggests an emotion.	I thoroughly explain how the images connect to the episodes and how each image suggests an emotion.
Presentation	My presentation of images and explanations lack neatness.	The images and attached explanations are clearly presented.	The images and attached explanations are presented neatly and effectively.

Reading Completed

Book Title: _____   Author: _____

❑ I have read the entire book.
❑ I have read at least half of the book.
❑ I have read less than half of the book.
❑ I have read little or none of the book.

What I like best about my pictures and explanations: _____
_____

My reading goal for next time: _____
_____

Picturing Textual Details

Book Title: *The Stolen Child*   Author: Keith Donohue

The first picture represents the setting, the place where the band of wild childlike beings is living. My illustration shows where most of the action in the book occurs.

The second picture establishes the moment in the book where Henry has been kidnapped. I illustrated this action because it is the conflict of the story. It shows the beginning of the challenges Henry must face.

The third and last picture shows how the band of the kidnappers and Henry have been bonding at the end of the story. Henry has become part of his captors' society.

Picturing Textual Details

Book Title: *The Search for Wondla*   Author: Tony DiTerlizzi

In this event, Eva Nine (the human) is on the ground, cowering because Rovender (the alien standing above Eva) had surprised Eva Nine by being angry and saw her omnipod fall out of her bag. Rovender picked up her omnipod, kept it and took it back to his sanctuary. This is a key event because later in the book Rovender becomes Eva's friend.

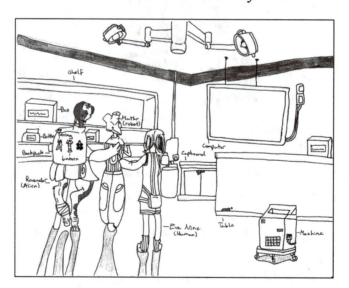

For this event, Rovender has become friends with Eva Nine and is helping her reboot her Muthr (her robotic parent or caretaker). He is taking Muthr to a lab where Muthr can be fixed. Eva hopes she can fix her Muthr and Eva is holding back her tears with all her might. This is a critical event because Muthr becomes one of the most important characters in the book.

Pembroke Publishers © 2012 *Ban the Book Report* by Graham Foster ISBN 978-1-55138-264-7

6 Assignments to Make Connections

Chapter 8 includes two additional connection assignments: Movie Actors to Play Major Characters (page 95) and A Song Related to My Book (page 99).

This section includes three assignments: connecting a book to personal experiences, connecting a book to other familiar texts, and reflecting on personal thought processes during the reading of a book.

Personal Connections is an appealing assignment for students who are willing to risk a detailed emotional response to reading. Teachers report that it is a popular choice among students. Many students appreciate the opportunity to connect textual details to events in their own lives.

Connecting My Book to Other Texts has proven to be challenging for students, certainly more challenging than connecting a book to one's personal experience. The assignment works best for voracious readers, as they are more capable of identifying a text that has similarities to their selected text. Note that one of the exemplars illustrates connecting a book to a video game.

Predictions and Questions as I Read focuses students on two powerful reading strategies: predicting and questioning. To be successful, students require instruction about why predictions and questions are important to readers. Teachers might recommend the assignment to students who could be more reflective about their reading strategies.

Personal Connections

Write about or talk about settings, events and/or people that your book reminded you of. Point out similarities and differences. As you present your personal reminders, include

1. similarities between your memories and selected details from your book
2. differences between your memories and selected details from your book
3. your emotional response to selected details from your book

Name: _____   Date: _____

	I'm not there yet	I'm getting there	I'm there now
Information about the Book	My response presents little or no detail about personal memories related to settings, events, or people in my book.	My response presents adequate detail about personal memories related to settings, events, or people related to my book.	My response presents extensive detail about personal memories of settings, events, or people related to my book.
Reasoning	My response includes little or no detail about my emotional response.	My response includes adequate detail about my emotional response.	My response includes extensive detail about my emotional response.
Presentation	My response is disorganized and not clearly worded. I am careless with spelling and grammar/usage.	My response is organized and clearly worded. A few mistakes with spelling and grammar/usage distract my reader.	My response is well-organized and effectively worded with few or no mistakes in spelling or grammar/usage.

Reading Completed

Book Title: _____   Author: _____

- ❑ I have read the entire book.
- ❑ I have read at least half of the book.
- ❑ I have read less than half of the book.
- ❑ I have read little or none of the book.

What I like best about my response: _____

_____

My reading goal for next time: _____

_____

Pembroke Publishers © 2012 *Ban the Book Report* by Graham Foster ISBN 978-1-55138-264-7

Personal Connections

Book Title: *Midnight Howl*   Author: Clare Hutton

The book reminds me of having to move from B.C. to Calgary and leave all my friends behind. But with Marisol, she had to move from Austin to Montana and leave all her friends. Unlike her, I didn't need to move in with people as we had to buy a house. Marisol had to move in with one of her mom's best friends from college. Her mom's friend had two kids that were twins. I just lived with my sisters and parents.

Another main similarity between my life and Marisol's occurred when she started to see that one of the twins, Haley, was acting really weird. Marisol thought that Haley was a werewolf. When she started to get scared, she would put her back to the door. Her room was right across from Haley's room. With me, I get scared a lot when I keep my door closed. I keep my door closed when I sleep after I watch a lot of scary movies.

The best part of the book that I felt really into was when Marisol had the dreams about the wolf hunting Marisol down and her waking up to it just being a dream. Afterwards she freaked out when she could not find Haley. It was a full moon and she heard howls. She went to her room and found that Haley was not in there and the window was open. I too fear dark, scary places. The book worked for me because it connected to my life on an emotional level.

Pembroke Publishers © 2012 *Ban the Book Report* by Graham Foster ISBN 978-1-55138-264-7

Personal Connections

Book Title: *Yakuza Moon*   Author: Shoko Tendo

My book's title is YAKUZA MOON, an autobiography of a girl named Shoko Tendo. She was the daughter of a yakuza, a gangster. This book tells about the ups and downs of her life, and sometimes it's really hard to believe what she has gone through. But I believe it's one book that you feel like you can connect to.

Some of the similarities between the book and my own life are how Shoko wants to fit in with the "crowd." She wants to be able to be like everyone around her especially her older sister. I know I've always wanted to fit in and be like everybody else—especially my sisters. But I finally discovered that you shouldn't have to fit in to be liked or do what everyone else does because you should be yourself. It doesn't matter if your friends dress the same or can draw or even have a boyfriend or girlfriend: you shouldn't have to follow everything that the people do around you. You should work and do things at your own pace. Don't look at what your friends do or how your sister or brother acts. Be yourself. This is exactly what the girl in the book came to realize.

The parts that were different in the book to my own life and memories are how Shoko took the wrong turns in life. Everybody makes mistakes in life but most of the time we realize that we made the mistakes and we try to fix them. But Shoko did not. It started with one little thing but that one little error grew bigger and bigger and started to snowball into a big mess and she didn't want to try to fix it. This is where I think she made a very big mistake. If she would have tried to fix it, I'm sure it would have been okay or at least better than what it was. Like me, I think a lot of people can relate to not doing anything about a problem. I'm realizing that you should always try to fix a problem before it starts to get out of hand and that's what I try to do.

I was really content to find that Shoko changed her life in the end of the book and was trying finally to fix the mistakes that she had made in the past. I really did not think that she would be able to fix everything that she did in the past, but it almost made me feel proud of her. YAKUZA MOON really impacted me and that's why I loved reading it.

Pembroke Publishers © 2012 *Ban the Book Report* by Graham Foster ISBN 978-1-55138-264-7

Connecting My Book to Other Texts

Write a few paragraphs to explain how your book is similar to other texts, including other books, movies, and TV programs. You might consider setting, characters, conflicts, subjects, and themes. Present specific details from the two texts to identify similarities and differences. Comment on whether you preferred your book or the related texts that you recall. Explain your preference.

Name: _____   Date: _____

	I'm not there yet	I'm getting there	I'm there now
Information about the Book	I present few or no details to compare and contrast my book and another text.	I adequately present details to compare and contrast my book and another text.	I thoroughly present details to compare and contrast my book and another text.
Reasoning	I provide little or no explanation about which text I prefer.	I present an adequate explanation abut which text I prefer.	I present a complete explanation about which text I prefer.
Presentation	My response is disorganized and not clearly worded. I am careless with spelling and grammar/usage.	My response is organized and clearly worded. A few mistakes with spelling and grammar/usage distract my reader.	My response is well-organized and effectively worded with few or no mistakes in spelling or grammar/usage.

Reading Completed

Book Title: _____   Author: _____

❑ I have read the entire book.
❑ I have read at least half of the book.
❑ I have read less than half of the book.
❑ I have read little or none of the book.

What I like best about my response: _____

_____

My reading goal for my next book: _____

_____

Pembroke Publishers © 2012 *Ban the Book Report* by Graham Foster ISBN 978-1-55138-264-7

Connecting My Book to Other Texts

Book Title: *The Lightning Thief*   Author : Rick Riordan
Compared to *Harry Potter and the Sorceror's Stone*   Author: J.K. Rowling

Peter Jackson of THE LIGHTNING THIEF has a lot in common with Harry Potter in HARRY POTTER AND THE SORCERER'S STONE. Their backgrounds, discoveries about themselves and their adventures have similarities.

Both Peter and Harry must deal with struggles when they are young. Peter seems to be dyslexic. He shares daily life with an abusive stepfather, Gabe Ugliano, whom he hates. He constantly gets into trouble at school and is expelled several times. Harry suffers bullying and neglect as he is raised by his aunt and uncle, Vernon and Petunia Dursley. He is especially persecuted by his cousin Dudley. Neither boy is particularly happy early in life.

Both Peter and Harry make amazing discoveries about their backgrounds. Percy discovers that he is the son of the Greek god, Poseidon, and that he himself is a demigod. As a boy, Harry discovers that he is a wizard. Once they discover the truth about their backgrounds, both boys engage in training. Peter trains to use his demigod powers. At Hogwarts, Harry Potter develops his skills in wizardry.

Both boys live through fantastic adventures with a major difference that Peter interacts with some famous characters of Greek mythology such as Hades and Persephone. Peter must use a map to locate Persephone's pearls and thereby escape from the underworld. Harry uses his invisibility cape to enter the three-headed dog's chamber. His quest is for the philosopher's stone that is supposed to contain the elixir of life.

Fortunately, both boys discover the power of friendship. Peter becomes comrades with Annabeth Chase and Luke Castellan. From them, he learns that teamwork is required to deal with life's challenges. Harry too, discovers friendship, especially with Ron Weasely who is "always there when you need him." Ron shows Harry that friends make sacrifices for friends. Without friends, Harry could not cope with his challenges.

Peter definitely reminds me of Harry. However, I do prefer THE LIGHTNING THIEF as a work of fantasy. It blends our current world with the world of Greek mythology. I've always been interested in Greek myths and my background helps me connect to Peter's adventures. Those who are less fond of Greek mythology will probably prefer Harry.

Pembroke Publishers © 2012 *Ban the Book Report* by Graham Foster ISBN 978-1-55138-264-7

Connecting My Book to Other Texts

Book Title: *Swordmage*　　　　　　　　　　　Author: Richard Baker
A Comparison of SWORDMAGE by Richard Baker and WARCRAFT (A Video Game)

SWORDMAGE, a novel by Richard Baker has similarities to WARCRAFT, a video game. The orcs (human-like creatures), the orc chieftains, the main character, the elves and the humans have similarities as well as a few differences that I'll highlight.

The orcs in SWORDMAGE are almost identical to the orcs in WARCRAFT except that in the book there is only one clan of orcs rather than the many different groups in the video game. While orcs in WARCRAFT are minor races, the orcs in SWORDMAGE are more prominent in the social order. However, the orcs in the novel have trouble working together. The hordes of orcs in WARCRAFT demonstrate the ability to work together under a single leader.

The orc chieftan in SWORDMAGE is a man named Mhurren who is half human. With his clan, he lives in a keep. While Mhurren is strong and cunning, he has no special magical powers. On the other hand, the orc warchief in WARCRAFT, Thrall, lives with his clan in a large settlement. Known as a "farseer," he has several magical abilities.

Garen Hulmaster, the major character in SWORDMAGE, has a natural sense of adventure. He decides to travel the world rather than to stay in his home town of Hulbury. Garen joins the service of the dragon shields where he earns a small fortune on quests. He is a successful trader. Jaina Proudmoore in WARCRAFT is not as focused on economic gain. However, like Garen, she shares a sense of adventure. She must travel to the far lands of Kalmidor to aid the night elves in the defeat of the Deamons and to prevent the lord destroyer from draining the world of its energies.

The elves in the book and the game are similar except that the elves in WARCRAFT are split into two factions—the high elves and the night elves. In SWORDMAGE, the elves are more like the high elves since they have the same abilities and live in a similar location. However, in the book the elves commanded enhanced magical powers compared to those in the game. They had the ability to use spells, to cast devastating blows, to teleport short distances and to shield themselves with magic.

In SWORDMAGE the humans control most of the world. The human kings are called harmachs and many smaller towns have no real leader. Some of the towns are controlled by major merchant companies and some by harmach and shieldsmen, the harmach's bodyguards. In WARCRAFT the humans are held together by the king and his court. Merchants form the middle class and farmers are quite common. The merchants do not have the political power in the towns. Both the novel and the game feature mages, humans with magical powers. In WARCRAFT, the mages are split into arch mages and blood mages. The mages in SWORDMAGE are closer to the blood mages since their focus is on inflicting damage.

Pembroke Publishers © 2012 *Ban the Book Report* by Graham Foster ISBN 978-1-55138-264-7

Exemplar continued

I prefer SWORDMAGE to WARCRAFT because the book features a very detailed plot with a few twists that keep you reading. With books, your mind makes the images. Richard Baker's descriptions create vivid images in my mind. Books tend to leave a lasting impression while video games just come and go.

Pembroke Publishers © 2012 *Ban the Book Report* by Graham Foster ISBN 978-1-55138-264-7

Predictions and Questions as I Read

Write about or talk about three predictions you made as you read your book, or three questions that you wondered about. Report how accurate your predictions were and what your predictions helped you learn or understand. Report on how your book answered the questions you wondered about. Remember that thoughtful predictions and questions often lead readers to important understandings.

Name: _____   Date: _____

	I'm not there yet	I'm getting there	I'm there now
Information about the Book	I do not explain how accurate my predictions were or how my questions were answered.	I provide some information about how accurate my predictions were or how my questions were answered.	I specifically indicate how accurate my predictions were or how my questions were answered.
Reasoning	I provide little or no explanation about what my predictions helped me to learn or to understand.	I provide a limited explanation abut what my predictions helped me to learn or to understand.	I clearly explain what my predictions helped me to learn or to understand.
Presentation	My response is disorganized and not clearly worded. I am careless with spelling and grammar/usage.	My response is organized and generally clear for my audience. A few mistakes with spelling and grammar/usage distract my reader.	My response is well-organized and clearly worded for my audience. There are few or no mistakes in spelling or grammar/usage.

Reading Completed

Book Title: _____   Author: _____

❑ I have read the entire book.
❑ I have read at least half of the book.
❑ I have read less than half of the book.
❑ I have read little or none of the book.

What I like best about my response: _____

_____

My reading goal for my next book: _____

_____

Pembroke Publishers © 2012 *Ban the Book Report* by Graham Foster ISBN 978-1-55138-264-7

Predictions and Questions as I Read

Book Title: *The Merchant of Venice: The Graphic Novel*   Author: Richard Appignanesi
(Adapted from Shakespeare's play)

This book is the story of a merchant from Venice named Bassanio. Bassanio meets a beautiful girl, Portia, and falls in love with her. In order for Bassanio to impress Portia, he needs money. Bassanio then borrows money from a rich banker named Shylock. Shylock lends money to Bassanio and his friends with a requirement of a pound of his human flesh if the money isn't paid back.

At the start of the book I was excited because of the magnificent graphics in it; the story showed Venice as it was hundreds of years ago. The conversations between the characters was a little hard to understand and read too. Still, I was dragged into the book. First I thought that Bassanio was very wealthy but it turned out to be opposite. I wondered what would happen to Bassanio—Would he win Portia's love? Would he be able to repay Shylock?

In the middle of the book, Bassanio completely falls in love with Portia, and Portia notices him and returns his love. I wondered if Portia looked so beautiful in real life that so many princes and gentlemen would want to marry her.

When Bassanio can't return the money that he borrowed from Shylock, he has a problem. Shylock brings Bassanio to extract a pound of flesh. I was so surprised by the court's judgment about Shylock's wish to take human flesh by cutting it from a guy's chest while being conscious. Dressed as a male lawyer, Portia saves Bassanio with an argument I hadn't predicted. Shylock may have his pound of flesh but may not draw blood since drawing blood was not in the contract! Who could predict that ending? It's easier to predict that Bossanio and Portia become a couple!

Pembroke Publishers © 2012 *Ban the Book Report* by Graham Foster ISBN 978-1-55138-264-7

Predictions And Questions As I Read

Book Title: *The Hunger Games: Catching Fire*   Author: Suzanne Collins

Suzanne Collins wrote CATCHING FIRE, the second book of the Hunger Games series. After reading a quarter of the book, I already had questions. Who is Plutarch Heavensbee? Was President Snow's decision about the games caused by the rebellion? Will Katniss' life end in this book? Predictions played in my head like alphabet soup. This book was unpredictable and breath-taking.

Once I started reading CATCHING FIRE, I couldn't stop. And then I came to the final chapter. I just couldn't read more unless I figured out what gave President Snow the idea to put the past victors back in the arena. After thinking about it, I concluded that President Snow knew about the rebellion even before Katniss did. Yes, President Snow must have known about the rebellion. As I read on, a thought came to me. The story suggested that President planned this whole victors' contest right in the beginning, during the first Hunger Games. I felt confused. Apparently the contest had nothing to do with the rebellion. It was planned before the rebellion even started. I was wrong in my prediction that the rebellion caused the victors' games.

Who is Plutarch Heavensbee? I know that he is a replacement of Seneca Crane, although he seemed to just come out of nowhere. He must have been part of it or led it. Since I wasn't sure, I read the book again. Plutarch was part of the rebellious group. He was silent and secretive, just waiting to make the right move to take on the face of the rebellion.

The lone question in my head that kept bugging me was "Will Katniss' life end here?" The question didn't make sense since I know the author could answer it in a later book. I didn't want the author to get rid of the main character, although Katniss' decisions made her look like a victim. Coming to the end of the book was intense for me. Katniss made alliances with the most incredible and unpredictable characters in the book. It felt that my prediction would be correct. This will be the end of Katniss' life. I was wrong. Plutarch saved her life. The book is so unpredictable that all you can do is wait and read.

I recommend CATCHING FIRE to both teenagers and adults. It keeps you questioning and predicting all the way through the book.

Pembroke Publishers © 2012 *Ban the Book Report* by Graham Foster ISBN 978-1-55138-264-7

7 Response to Informational Text

This section includes a reading response option for informational or nonfiction texts. While many students prefer fiction for free-time teaching, those who are interested in a specific topic willingly read informational text. Nonfiction should certainly be an option in extensive reading programs.

Interesting Features of an Information Book focuses on why readers enjoy informational texts—to answer important question and to learn about topics of personal interest. Teachers might choose to let students use a magazine article to complete the assignment. Students motivated to read informational text are able to manage the open-ended format of the assignment.

Interesting Features of an Informational Book

After reading a book that presents factual information about a topic of personal interest, write or talk about three or four questions the book answers for you. Remember that your reader or listener has probably not read the book. As you present your response to others, specify

1. Questions the book answered for you
2. Additional interesting information in the text
3. Why you find the information helpful and other questions you wonder about

Name: _____   Date: _____

	I'm not there yet	I'm getting there	I'm there now
Information about the Book	I present little or no information related to three or four questions that my book helped me answer, or about interesting information in the text.	I present adequate information related to three or four questions that my book helped me answer, and about interesting information in the text.	I present detailed information related to three of four questions that my book helped me answer, and about interesting information in the text.
Reasoning	I provide little or no explanation about why I found the information useful and interesting.	I adequately explain why I found the information useful and interesting	I thoroughly explain why I found the information useful and interesting
Presentation	My response is disorganized and not clearly for my audience. I am careless with spelling and grammar/usage.	My response is organized and generally clear for my audience. A few mistakes with spelling and grammar/usage distract my reader.	My response is well-organized and consistently clear for my audience. There are few or no mistakes in spelling or grammar/usage.

Reading Completed

Book Title: _____   Author: _____

- ❑ I have read the entire book.
- ❑ I have read at least half of the book.
- ❑ I have read less than half of the book.
- ❑ I have read little or none of the book.

What I like best about my response: _____

_____

My reading goal for my next book: _____

_____

Pembroke Publishers © 2012 *Ban the Book Report* by Graham Foster ISBN 978-1-55138-264-7

Interesting Features of an Informational Book

Book Title: *A Really Short History of Nearly Everything*   Author: Bill Bryson

Have you ever really given a thought about the origins of our universe? You may say it all started with the big bang and it quite possibly did. Now the question is why that happened and what happened afterwards. Both are questions I gave thought of before picking up A REALLY SHORT HISTORY OF NEARLY EVERYTHING. It was the back of the book that really caught me. Five questions……Right in the middle of the list was the question "How heavy is the earth?" How heavy is the earth? I thought that was a good question.

I started the book. At first I learned why Bill Bryson wrote the book—not what I was looking for. Then I turned the page. There, staring right at me was the first question set, "What is the big bang?… Why not the small bang or the no bang? What was the big bang and why did it occur?" Of course, it was only a theory, but a quite plausible theory. The theory stated that before the big bang, everything that is anything was squished up inside a space smaller than a zillionth of a proton. Suddenly an explosion occurred involving everything that is to be is created. All matter, every atom, in every body, every atom in existence has now come to be following the big bang. This of course opened up more questions. How could our unimaginable, tremendously gigantic universe fit into such an unimaginably tiny space? How? At the bottom of the page was another amazing fact. Before the big bang, time did not exist. Time didn't exist! The very reality that runs our clockwork lives did not exist! Time equaled zero.

I continued reading, hoping to discover the answer to my second question. "What happened after the big bang?" I knew we humans wouldn't be appearing for quite awhile but I wanted to know not about human history, not even ancient history. I wanted to know about history that played out just after the big bang. Conveniently, my search wasn't long. Soon after reading that time equaled zero, I found what I was looking for. Three minutes after the big bang, gravity and other forces that govern our day to day lives, emerged; then came stupendous heat—so hot it could cause nuclear reactions. After that most of everything that ever will be existed. Gravity soon began creating brilliant spirals of gas and dust that would become the worlds' stars as well as gathering various left over rubble to create planets. One of those swirls would become our sun and a clump of rock our earth. Once earth came into being life could spring forth. That though would take an awfully long time. Explaining everything that happened after earth was created would take me too long to write. Along my journey through A REALLY SHORT HISTORY OF NEARLY EVERYTHING, I came across a fact I found slightly terrifying. It stated that if I happened to pick myself apart atom by atom, I would produce a great pile of atoms of which none had ever been alive. Thankfully, I found a much more pleasant fact that every atom was probably part of a star once upon a time.

Pembroke Publishers © 2012 *Ban the Book Report* by Graham Foster ISBN 978-1-55138-264-7

Exemplar continued

The rest of the book told of much that happened after the big bang. I discovered a myriad of facts of which I had no previous knowledge. I continued my journey until I discovered a much more interesting section. "How heavy is the earth?" By then my question had changed slightly. Not only did I want to know how much the earth weighed, but also how big it was. The first page said at the top "Measuring the Earth." Excited, I began to read. By the end of the page, I learned about triangulation to measure the earth…. This number I soon learned wasn't quite accurate. It took me six pages to discover the answer. Mostly, I realized that measuring the earth was quite a complicated task. The earth it turns out isn't perfectly round, this making the measurement quite tricky. The earth was approximately 26,280 miles around.

Next came the question of the earth's weight. After four pages explaining calculations, brilliant ideas, delicate experiments and complicated machines, I found the answer. The earth weighs approximately 5,972 zillion, trillion tonnes. How ever, I wondered, could Atlas carry the weight on his shoulders!

After my questions were answered, I persisted. My head is now filled with mind boggling information such as the fact sixty percent of human genes are the same as those of a fruit fly and that human existence has lasted than one percent of the trilobite's existence. By the end of the book many of my questions were answered, but these questions had been replaced with new question. What tremendous insights will be discovered in the near future?

Pembroke Publishers © 2012 *Ban the Book Report* by Graham Foster ISBN 978-1-55138-264-7

Interesting Features of an Informational Book

Book Title: *Classical Mythology*   Author: William Hanson

What's likeable and unlikeable about Aphrodite?

There aren't many likeable things about Aphrodite, but some of her appealing qualities include that she is very generous. For example, she let Hera borrow her very own special weapon—the battle glove cestus. Another positive asset is that she is very beautiful, a reason that many people respected her. The unlikeable features about her are that she is disloyal because she had an affair with Ares, even though she was married to Hephaestus. Another negative out of many is that she severely punishes those who think they are better than she is or anybody who dares not to worship her.

Interesting Information about Aphrodite: In the Greek tradition, Aphrodite is the daughter of Zeus and Dione. Her special weapon is the cestus, a glove that makes the wearer more attractive. She is also one of the twelve Olympians and is in the younger generation of gods.

What's likeable and unlikeable about Hera?

Just like Aphrodite, Hera doesn't have much to like about her either. Her unlikeable attributes are that she is an extremely jealous person and also very resentful. However, to her credit she is also very faithful to her allies.

Interesting Information about Hera: Even though she is Zeus' sister, she is still presently married to him, and has borne his three children. Her status among the gods is to be the queen of the gods, and she is one of the elder Olympians. Her father is Kronos and her mother is Rhea of the Titans.

I liked this book because I wanted to learn more about Greek mythology. It answered how the Olympians were born and which heroes, minor gods, and monsters they created. It's also kind of amusing to see the strange, unusual and sometimes cruel punishments meted out by Greek gods.

Pembroke Publishers © 2012 *Ban the Book Report* by Graham Foster ISBN 978-1-55138-264-7

Creating Your Own Reading-Response Assignments

The preceding part of the book illustrates personally significant reading-response options for students. The 20 assignments might be useful models for teachers to create a range of other motivational reading response tasks.

This part of the book includes one chapter:

8 Work in Progress for Reading-Response Assignments

As a professional development activity, a group of teachers reviewed the 20 assignments presented in this book and chose the goal to develop parallel reading-response assignments—tasks that offered varied personally significant options, each with a rubric written in student-friendly language and each with illustrative exemplars. In a day, the group successfully developed eight assignments, each with a rubric. Teachers left the workshop with the intention of gathering exemplars for the eight assignments.

The professional development model chosen by these teachers serves as a useful model:

1. Develop motivational reading-response assignments.
2. Develop a rubric in student-friendly language.
3. Collect exemplars for the reading-response assignments.
4. Share the assignments, rubrics, and exemplars with colleagues.

The following pages illustrate the first part of their work—the generation of reading assignments and the development of rubrics— for the following assignments:

- Movie Actors to Play Major Characters
- Create a Social Media Page
- Write a Poem
- Award Certificate for the Author
- A Song Related to My Book
- Scrapbook or Backpack Collection
- Create and Perform a Dramatic Script
- Readers' Theatre

Movie Actors to Play Major Characters

List two or three major characters in your novel or biography. Identify three or four characters traits for each of these characters. Choose an actor who would convincingly portray your character. Provide reasons for your choice—possibly identifying the actor's previous roles as characters similar to those in you book.

Name: _____   Date: _____

	I'm not there yet	I'm getting there	I'm there now
Information about the Book	I do not specify any required character traits.	I specify some character traits but need to be more complete.	I clearly specify three or four traits for each major character.
Reasoning	I need to add reasons to explain my choice of actor for each main character.	I provide adequate reasons to explain my choice of actor for each major character.	I provide thorough reasoning to explain my choice of actor for each major character.
Presentation	My word choice is imprecise. I am careless with spelling and grammar/usage.	My word choice is accurate. A few mistakes with spelling and grammar/usage distract my reader.	My word choice is precise and effective. I have few or no mistakes in spelling and grammar/usage.

Create a Social Media Page

Create a social media page for a major character in your novel or biography. Major headings should reveal important personal information about the character, information that the character would like to share with potential Internet friends. Headings might include the following:

- Work and Education
- Family Background
- Current and Previous Locations
- Personal History by Year
- Important Beliefs
- Contact Information
- Likes and Dislikes

1. Provide important details in at least five categories so that the reader gets a sense of the character's life and values.
2. Add a paragraph to explain the two most important details that you have included in the page.

Name: _____   Date: _____

	I'm not there yet	I'm getting there	I'm there now
Information about the Book	I include very limited information about my major character.	I include adequate information about my major character.	I include detailed information about my major character.
Reasoning	I provide little or no reasoning to explain the two most important details that I have included.	I provide adequate reasoning to explain the two most important details that I have included.	I provide thorough reasoning to explain the two most important details that I have included.
Presentation	My word choice is imprecise. I am careless with spelling and grammar/usage.	My word choice is accurate. A few mistakes with spelling and grammar/usage distract my reader.	My word choice is precise and effective. I have few or no mistakes in spelling and grammar/usage.

Pembroke Publishers © 2012 *Ban the Book Report* by Graham Foster ISBN 978-1-55138-264-7

Write a Poem

Poems frequently capture an emotional experience and suggest ideas about that powerful experience. Think about a key event in your novel—an event that has major impact on a major character.

1. To plan your writing of a poem to capture the experience, list the details that will help the reader understand the event. Consider details related to the five senses: sight, hearing, touch, taste, and smell.
2. Draft your poem.
3. In revision, check that you have presented details that capture the emotion of the experience. Check that you have included words that suggest the emotion.

Name: _____   Date: _____

	I'm not there yet	I'm getting there	I'm there now
Information about the Book	The reader is unsure about my poem's emotional experience.	My poem suggests an emotional experience.	My poem clearly suggests an emotional experience.
Detail	My poem lacks details that suggest an emotional experience.	My poem includes details that suggest an emotional experience.	My poem includes details that strongly suggest an emotional experience.
Presentation	My work choice is imprecise. I am careless with my spelling and grammar/usage.	My word choice is accurate. A few mistakes with spelling and grammar/usage distract my reader.	My word choice is precise and effective. I have few or no mistakes in spelling and grammar/usage.

Award Certificate for the Author

Complete a web search for award certificates. Locate examples that furnish the following information:

- the organization presenting the award
- the accomplishment
- the name of recipient
- reasons for the award
- official signature

Locate examples that are visually appealing because of logos, visual images, and borders or lettering.

Create an award certificate for an author. Include all of the information listed above.

Name: _____   Date: _____

	I'm not there yet	I'm getting there	I'm there now
Features of Award Certificate	My award certificate includes few critical features of an effective award.	My award certificate includes most of the critical features of an effective award certificate.	My award certificate includes all of the critical features of an effective award certificate.
Presentation	My award certificate lacks neatness and visual appeal.	My award certificate is neat but could be more visually appealing.	My award certificate is neat and visually appealing.

Pembroke Publishers © 2012 *Ban the Book Report* by Graham Foster ISBN 978-1-55138-264-7

A Song Related to My Book

Think of important details of the setting, characters, and plot of your book. Choose a song that connects to some of these details. Write two or three paragraphs to explain similarities and differences between your book and your selected song. Comment on whether you preferred the book or the song. Explain your preference.

Name: _____   Date: _____

	I'm not there yet	I'm getting there	I'm there now
Information about the Book	I present few or no details to compare and contrast my book and my song.	I adequately present details to compare and contrast my book and my song.	I thoroughly present details to compare and contrast my book and my song.
Reasoning	I present an imprecise explanation about why I prefer my book or the song.	I present an adequate explanation about why I prefer the book or the song.	I present a complete explanation about why I prefer the book or the song.
Presentation	My word choice is imprecise. I am careless with my spelling and grammar/usage.	My word choice is accurate. A few mistakes with spelling and grammar/usage distract my reader.	My word choice is precise and effective. I have few or no mistakes in spelling and grammar/usage.

Pembroke Publishers © 2012 *Ban the Book Report* by Graham Foster ISBN 978-1-55138-264-7

Scrapbook or Backpack Collection

For one of the characters in your novel, list items that would be included in the character's scrapbook or backpack. With your teacher's guidance, decide whether you will simply complete the list or will create the scrapbook or actually place items in a backpack. In either case, provide a brief explanation of your choices. If you do create an actual scrapbook or backpack collection, you can challenge classmates to examine your work to identify your selected character.

Name: _____   Date: _____

	I'm not there yet	I'm getting there	I'm there now
Information about the Book	I present a limited list or collection of items.	I present an adequate list or collection items.	I present a complete list or collection of items.
Reasoning	I offer few or no reasons to explain how my list or collection relates to my character.	I adequately explain why my list or collection relates to my character.	I thoroughly explain why my list or collection relates to my character.
Presentation	My word choice is imprecise. I am careless with my spelling and grammar/usage.	My word choice is accurate. A few mistakes with spelling and grammar/usage distract my reader.	My word choice is precise and effective. I have few or no mistakes in spelling and grammar/usage.

Create and Perform a Dramatic Script

Working on your own, or in a small group with students who have all read your novel or biography, create and perform a dramatic script based on the text.

1. Locate a brief section of text that is noteworthy for its presentation of conflict between or among characters.
2. Rewrite the text as a dramatic script.
3. With your teacher's advice, decide whether you will read the text or present a memorized version to classmates.
4. As your group performs the script, focus on revealing the characters' feelings and the effect of the conflict.

Name: _____ Date: _____

	I'm not there yet	I'm getting there	I'm there now
Selection of Text	The text we performed contains little or no conflict.	Some of the text we performed illustrates conflict.	All of the text we performed illustrates conflict.
Volume and Pacing	We make little attempt to use volume and pacing to emphasize conflict.	We use volume and pacing to emphasize the conflict.	We effectively use volume and pacing to emphasize the conflict.
Clarity of Expression	We need to speak more clearly and to pause more appropriately.	We sometimes speak clearly and pause appropriately.	We consistently speak clearly and pause appropriately.
Emphasis	Our presentation provides little or no indication of the point of highest emotional intensity.	Our presentation provides some indication of the point of highest emotional intensity.	Our presentation clearly builds to the point of highest emotional intensity.

Pembroke Publishers © 2012 *Ban the Book Report* by Graham Foster ISBN 978-1-55138-264-7

Readers' Theatre

In a readers' theatre presentation, your main challenge is to employ voice to suggest a character's thoughts, feelings, responses, and conflict.

1. Select a section of your novel or biography that is especially dramatic or focused on conflict.
2. Work in a group to discuss characters' feelings, responses, and motivations in the section you have selected.
3. Decide on who will read what section of text as you perform the text for classmates. Decide whether you need someone to read the non-dialogue parts.
4. Practice different ways of saying the text to discover the best way to use volume, pacing, and intonation to reveal characters' feelings.

Name: _____   Date: _____

	I'm not there yet	I'm getting there	I'm there now
Selection of Text	The text we performed has little or no conflict.	Some of the text we performed illustrates conflict.	All of the text we performed illustrates conflict.
Volume and Pacing	We make little attempt to use volume and pacing to emphasize conflict.	We use volume and pacing to emphasize the conflict.	We effectively use volume and pacing to emphasize conflict.
Clarity of Expression	We need to speak more clearly and to pause more appropriately.	We sometimes speak clearly and pause appropriately.	We consistently speak clearly and pause appropriately.
Emphasis	Our presentation provides little or no indication of the point of highest emotional intensity.	Our presentation provides some indication of the point of highest emotional intensity.	Our presentation clearly builds to the point of highest emotional intensity.

Collecting Exemplars for Reading-Response Assignments

Exemplars featured in the assignments illustrate student-centered, motivational alternatives to analytical book reports. Over the past several years, teachers have collected exemplars to set standards for writing and to instruct students about effective writing. Like other exemplars, exemplars of student responses to independent reading provide powerful instructional resources for teachers and students.

As you develop assignments, consider how you plan to use exemplars. Will the exemplars be used in classes from which they are collected? Will the exemplars be anonymous? Will the exemplars be posted in the classroom? Many teachers collect exemplars for use with other classes in subsequent years. In addition, many teachers choose to present exemplars anonymously. With these approaches, the instructional focus is placed on the work rather than on the person who created the work. The posting of exemplars furnishes students with a handy reference as they complete reading-response assignments.

Teachers should respect privacy laws and school district guidelines for the collection and instructional use of student work. Teachers might require parental permission. Modify the letter and permission slip on page 104 to more clearly reflect local privacy laws and school district guidelines.

Dear _____:

I would like to use the attached reading-response assignment as an educational resource. Such samples are useful in instructing and motivating students.

Consistent with district guidelines, I request your approval for use of the attached assignment. If you agree to this use, please sign and return the following permission form.

I have already received your child's permission to use the work sample to help other students learn. Please be assured that your child's work will be presented anonymously and will be honored as an instructional resource.

If you have questions or concerns please call me at _____.

_____
Signature

— —

Permission Form

Date: _____

I grant permission for _____ School to use the attached work sample as an instructional resource for other students.

_____
Signature of Parent or Guardian

Pembroke Publishers © 2012 *Ban the Book Report* by Graham Foster ISBN 978-1-55138-264-7

Conclusion

Reflecting on Reading Response in Our School

Use the checklist on page 107 to begin discussion about collaborative action to improve your school's extensive reading program.

The checklist on page 107 might help you and your colleagues decide on an action plan to increase the amount of independent reading completed by students in your school and to ensure that reading-response assignments promote frequent and enthusiastic reading.

Ban the Book Report began as a year-long professional development project in two schools. Teachers collaborated on an action plan related to the criteria on the checklist. Students in these schools knew that some of their reading responses would be published in this book. However, whether or not their work was selected, students reported enthusiasm for the reading-response options. Project teachers noted a significant increase in the amount of extensive reading completed by students in the two schools.

Teachers who subscribe to the methodology illustrated here will continue to develop and present assignments that encourage rather than discourage reading. They will offer reading-response options that relate to students' interests and to their emotional response to text. They will furnish opportunities for oral and dramatic responses, as well as opportunities to illustrate and represent text. Yes, let's ban the book report. Let's develop and refine reading-response options that encourage students to love reading and to read frequently for the rest of their lives.

Acknowledgments

The author gratefully acknowledges advice and assistance from the following individuals:

- Valerie Viccars, Assistant Manager, Services for Children, Teens and Families, Calgary Public Library
- Jeannette MacDonald, Language Arts Consultant, Calgary Catholic Schools
- Janeen Werner-King, Professional Learning Community Learning Leader, Calgary Board of Education
- the administration, librarian, and humanities teachers of H.D. Cartwright Public School, Calgary, Alberta: Mary Ellen Dewar, Stephen Moses, Andrea Byrne, Judy Young-Davis, Nzingha Austin-Joyner, Brenda Borgeson, Lesley Scullion, Tammy Jeffrey, Kim Boucher, Jamie-Dee Peterson, and Pat Teslak
- the administration, librarian, and language arts teachers of Bishop Kidd Separate School, Calgary, Alberta: Mark Macgillivray, Stephen Jez, Jo-Ann

MacNeil, Heather Gallagher, Andrea Slough, Jennifer Patoine, and Catherine Grant
- Susan Lee, Killam Public School, Killam, Alberta
- Cherisse Audet, Ecole St. Gérard, Calgary, Alberta.

In addition, the author thanks the students whose reading responses have been included in the book and their parents for granting permission for publication of their children's work.

Suggested Sources

Books

Good Books Matter, Shelley Stagg Peterson and Larry Schwartz (2008), provides a useful list of recommended books, selection strategies for specific grade levels, instructional suggestions, assignments, and assessment.

Book Crush, Nancy Pearl (2007), lists more than 1,000 titles for children of all ages organized under three broad headings: Youngest Readers, Middle Grade Readers, and Teen Readers.

Best Books for Kids and Teens, published annually by the Canadian Children's Book Centre, recommends Canadian books, novels, audio, and video for children and teens. The resource offers useful information about interest level, grade level, and thematic fit. In addition, the Canadian Children's Book Centre website offers valuable information to parents and teachers about guiding young people to appropriate books.

Journals

School Library Journal
Publishers Weekly
These journals have websites that teachers and librarians can view without a subscription. Around December or January, these journals publish lists of the best books of the year.

Web Resources

Canadian Review of Materials, or *CM*, is an electronic reviewing journal published every Friday from September to June. It provides book reviews, author profiles, news about awards, and recommended titles.

Reading Rants is a blog that features the recommendations of middle school librarian Jennifer Hubert.

Guys Read, created by author Jon Scieszka, features books for boys recommended by boys.

A Checklist for Reflection on Reading Response in Our School

❏   1. Our students enjoy access to a wide collection of appealing books, including graphic novels and recorded books.

❏   2. Our students have the opportunity to hear texts read aloud.

❏   3. Our students spend class time reading books of their own choosing.

❏   4. Our students select their own books for extensive reading.

❏   5. Most students in our school read at least one book per month.

❏   6. Our school plans celebrations of reading.

❏   7. Our school offers reading-response assignments connected to students' interests and to their emotional response to text.

❏   8. Our school includes oral and dramatic interpretation as reading-response options.

❏   9. Our school includes illustration and representation as reading-response options.

❏ 10. Our school provides assignment-specific rubrics for reading-response assignments.

❏ 11. Our school employs exemplars to illustrate expectations and possibilities for reading responses.

Pembroke Publishers © 2012 *Ban the Book Report* by Graham Foster ISBN 978-1-55138-264-7

Index